D1250177

Bond Book

This book is one of 155,000 in a special purchase to upgrade the CALS collection. Funds for the project were approved by Little Rock voters on 8/17/04.

If you never had the unspeakable privilege of knowing Nancy, you will feel as if you did by the end of this book. And, like the author, you will be the richer for it.

JERRY B. JENKINS—Coauthor, Left Behind Series

I didn't linger Over Salad and Hot Bread; *I devoured it. Written with honesty and humility, Mary will inspire and nourish whether you're thinking about life or death.*

MARY GRAHAM—President, Women of Faith

Reading this book felt very much like a visit to Jan Karon's imaginary town of Mitford and meeting two women who go to Father Tim's church. What a privilege we have as readers to enter into their unlikely friendship and connect to their very real lives. You'll come away yearning for the kind of relationship that Mary and Nancy shared. This book is truly outstanding.

BARBARA RAINEY—Cofounder, FamilyLife; Author; Speaker

Over Salad and Hot Bread *is more than a "how to" on generational friendship; it's an honest expression of the grace that passed between these two women. As Mary says, "Nancy helped me live, and I helped her die. Our friendship made us better."*

VICKI BENTLEY—Speaker; Women's Ministry Leader, Maranatha Chapel, San Diego, California

Mary Jenson's beautiful portrait of friendship will inspire you to venture out of your comfort zone to discover an intimacy that will draw the very best out of each willing soul.

DARCY J. KIMMEL—Author; Speaker; Cofounder,
Family Matters

Some books leave you entertained or even moved. This one leaves you longing to engage in authentic friendship and to ultimately experience the koinonia *that God has intended for us all along.*

CHERYL RECCORD—Coauthor, *Launching Your Kids for Life*;
Speaker; Founder and President, Total Life Impact, Inc.

The richness of this writing will make you laugh, cry and identify with the longings and fears in your own life. You'll be captivated by fresh insights into really living *and* gracefully dying—*both with a deep sense of joy.*

SUSAN ALEXANDER YATES—Best-Selling Author of
several books, including *And Then I Had Teenagers* and
Encouragement for Parents of Teens and Preteens.

This book captures the heart and beauty of women mentoring women and opens our eyes to the blessings of aging. We can all learn something from this sensitive account of these two women.

TONI FORTSON—Speaker; Author;
Wife of President of Promise Keepers

foreword by Jerry B. Jenkins

what an old friend taught me about life

over salad&
hot bread

mary jenson

HOWARD
PUBLISHING CO.

Our purpose at Howard Publishing is to:

• *Increase faith* in the hearts of growing Christians

• *Inspire holiness* in the lives of believers

• *Instill hope* in the hearts of struggling people everywhere

Because He's coming again!

Over Salad and Hot Bread © 2006 by Mary Jenson
All rights reserved. Printed in the United States of America
Published by Howard Publishing Co., Inc.
3117 North Seventh Street, West Monroe, Louisiana 71291-2227

06 07 08 09 10 11 12 13 14 15   10 9 8 7 6 5 4 3 2 1

Edited by Cheryl Dunlop
Interior design by John Mark Luke Designs
Cover design by Terry Dugan

Library of Congress Cataloging-in-Publication Data

Jenson, Mary.
    Over salad & hot bread : what an old friend taught me about life / Mary Jenson.
        p. cm.
    ISBN 1-58229-495-X
    1. Female friendship—Religious aspects—Christianity. 2. Christian women—Religious
life. 3. Jenson, Mary. 4. Bayless, Nancy. I. Title: Over salad and hot bread. II. Title.

BV4527.J46 2006
241'.6762—dc22

                                                                          2006041056

No part of this publication may be reproduced in any form without the prior written
permission of the publisher except in the case of brief quotations within critical articles
and reviews.

Scripture quotations not otherwise marked are from the *Holy Bible, New International
Version*® NIV®. Copyright © 1973, 1978, 1984 by International Bible Society. Used by
permission of Zondervan. All rights reserved. Scripture quotations marked NKJV are from
the *New King James Version*®. Copyright © 1982 by Thomas Nelson, Inc. Used by permission. All rights reserved. Italics in Scripture quotations indicate author's added emphasis.

to Nancy Bayless:

(After all, who knows what
that "great cloud of witnesses" can hear or see?)
I hope you're hanging around
and will find a way to keep me in line.
You really did leave a mark on me,
and I don't want to ever forget it.

and
to Vicki Bentley
and Jennie Gillespie:

You're Nancy's and my "other half."
This is your story too.

CENTRAL ARKANSAS LIBRARY SYSTEM
ADOLPHINE FLETCHER TERRY BRANCH
LITTLE ROCK, ARKANSAS

contents

contents

foreword

The beauty of Mary Jenson's homage to her friend—or more accurately to her friendship with—Nancy Bayless is that she avoids deifying the woman. When one has a special friend, as so many of us considered Nancy, it would be easy to fall into hagiography and idolization.

Nancy—I called her Tess (you'll see why in Mary's account)—could be feisty and blunt and loving and opinionated and selfless, almost all at the same time. She had an ability to endear herself to strangers immediately.

And yet Mary, who during her own midlife became a fast friend to Nancy, is able to sort through the many-faceted personality of the unique woman of the harbor. By being self-revelatory and introspective, Mary somehow makes this account a coming-of-middle-age story that transcends nostalgia and becomes instructive to us all.

One of my favorite memories of Nancy was when she and my wife and I and seven others went looking for dessert late one night during a conference. Everyone ordered some sinful concoction; everyone, that is, except Nancy, who insisted she simply shouldn't and couldn't and wouldn't. Then, of course, she proceeded to mooch "just a taste" of everyone else's.

Friends of Nancy will recognize her in that anecdote. But if you never had the unspeakable privilege of knowing her, you will feel as if you did by the end of this book. And, like the author, you will be the richer for it.

—Jerry B. Jenkins

acknowledgments

My deepest thanks to you, Jennie, for putting so much aside, including your own writing, to help me with mine. In case you're inclined to forget it, we're a team from now on, like it or not.

To Kathy, Johnny, and Cristina, and the rest of Nancy's family I didn't know: thank you for letting me write this personal account without spending many words on you, whom she loved most.

To the army of Nancy's friends at Maranatha Chapel, Shelter Island, and elsewhere (if you think this might include you, it does): You were sweet oil on Nancy's head. Thank you particularly for all you did for her in her last days. Had I any chance of knowing or remembering *all* your names, I would mention you one by one.

To Chip MacGregor: Thank you for championing this project when it was just a few little anecdotes. Your encouragement is priceless to me.

To Cheryl Dunlop: I knew from your first e-mail, so well written and properly punctuated, that I could trust your copy-editing skills! Thank you for flexing with my schedule.

And to Howard Publishing and Philis Boultinghouse: Thank you for "just plain liking this" on the basis of a few pages and half an idea. Nancy would have loved meeting you guys, I can tell.

Therefore, since we are surrounded by such a great cloud of witnesses, let us throw off everything that hinders and the sin that so easily entangles, and let us run with perseverance the race marked out for us.

—HEBREWS 12:1

introduction:
a simple story of friendship

I don't suppose, unless it's tied to your occupation, you ever get used to being in the room with a dead person. But when you've been there for the dying process and done what you could do and said what you needed to say, it's not so bad.

Three of us stood at Nancy's feet—Vicki, Jennie, and I—we who had spent so much time with her in the months of her dying. Her little apartment had become such a familiar place to us, and, thankfully, not a dismal place. That vanilla scent she'd insisted on spraying around the room day after day lingered in the air. It was a gift to us as much as to herself.

Nancy and I had a few years to learn how to be friends and just a few months to learn how to die. But this book is not about death. It's about life and friendship and what she taught me.

One year before Nancy died, we were nearing the end of a car trip and having lunch at a cliffside restaurant overlooking the Pacific. We'd come from a writers' conference, where she had won a lifetime-achievement award for her work mentoring young writers. We were high on inspiration and moved by having shared the week's experience. And Nancy, not one to rest on her laurels, was ready to write—and mentor—again.

Over salad and hot bread she posed the question: "Why don't we write a book together?"

"About what?" I couldn't imagine.

"About friendship. About what puts a classy young chick like you together with an adventurous old soul like me. About how much we love our car trips and how much fun we have with each other."

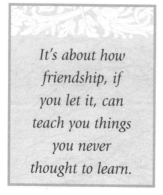

It's about how friendship, if you let it, can teach you things you never thought to learn.

Skeptical at first that we'd have anything to say, I decided after all I loved the idea and the challenge. We chortled over our salads, speculated about a possible book tour and an appearance on *Oprah*, brainstormed on a title, and scratched down ideas. We set a few goals and gave ourselves some deadlines. There was no sense of urgency. We had all the time in the world.

But we were wrong. The lump in her breast, which she had chosen to ignore, took its own trip and spread throughout her body with great speed, surprising us all.

A week before she died, Nancy and I looked at each other and said simultaneously, "I'm so sorry we haven't finished." We had

introduction: a simple story of friendship

wanted our book to be a give-and-take discussion about friendship between generations. But though the direction changed and I ended up doing most of the work, I was comforted by something Nancy once said (and I'm so glad I wrote it down): "The best thing about our relationship is that we write together like one mind. Often we don't remember whose words are whose. And it doesn't matter. It just doesn't matter."

So in the end, this is my version of our story, with some of our conversations and her writing sprinkled in. We were women in different stages of life with very different backgrounds who happened upon each other. We had no grandiose purpose for spending time together. Just a common love of books and good writing, a passionate faith, and a fondness for each other.

I thought it would be a simple story of friendship. It is. But it's also about how friendship, if you let it, can teach you things you never thought to learn.

i was the driver; nancy,
the supply sergeant

I couldn't believe it. Here I was, late-forty-something, back in those old high-school insecurities, wondering if I fit in, wondering if I had the right clothes, wondering if I'd have to share a bed with this "girl" I hardly knew.

That's where it all began, in a conference-center bedroom in the Colorado mountains in the fall of 1997. I'd joined a small group of friends for a writers' conference in Winter Park, my old skiing grounds. I loved being in the mountains again, with the glittering aspens and the sky so clear and brittle that a simple shout might shatter it. The bitter cold crept down our necks, keeping us clustered together like frozen grapes on a stem.

As the newest member of this little group, I wanted to belong, wanted to be in the middle of things rather than on the periphery. I knew Jennie and Vicki (my contemporaries) well, but Nancy was a newer friend; so when we got our room assignments and I found I'd been paired with her, I was silently disappointed.

We were two generations of woman, Nancy and I. We called ourselves friends, but I hadn't taken the time to invest much in our relationship. After all, I still had kids at home the age of her grandchildren. I was busy, involved, heavily scheduled. And from what I could tell, there wasn't much to connect us.

I was feeling shy and self-conscious, wondering if things would be uncomfortably quiet in our room, wanting to do this right. Did Nancy care which bed she slept in? Did little old ladies have any idiosyncrasies I should anticipate?

So I asked her what she wanted in a roommate. It took her a minute. Finally, she said, "Just keep the sink clean." Believe me, I watched every hair that drifted onto the porcelain, sweeping it out before it had time to get comfortable.

It didn't take me long to relax. Nancy put me at ease and, like a magnet, drew the other girls into our room. I quickly discovered she was the party girl, the one you needed to be with when you were feeling shy.

And she was so easy to please. Just keep the sink clean, give her a cozy bunk, and stop asking if she's all right.

Nestled under the covers one evening, Nancy and I scratched

> *The bitter cold crept down our necks, keeping us clustered together like frozen grapes on a stem.*

away on our notepads at some personal reflections. It was the first time she'd been away from her ailing husband for more than a few hours, and I knew she was thinking about him. She wrote steadily, with intense focus, under the kind of inspiration you don't want to let go of until every last word is out. When she finished, we read to each other.

This is what she was working on:

Sometimes I want to scream! It's devastating to watch the mental deterioration of my strong, tall, gentle husband. My stern and splendid mate. His fine mind is off somewhere . . . frolicking through autumn leaves, I like to think. It comes home when I least expect it, to amaze me with its intellect, logic, and humor that never sleeps. Then it scurries away again, leaving me with tears splashing on my bare toes.

Sometimes I want to giggle when I see him getting into bed . . . fully clothed! His hat cocked with jaunty defiance. His wallet and car keys tucked in the side pockets of his jeans. Though he hasn't started a car for years, he keeps his keys ready to open the driver's door for me and pat me in with gallant care. And he always reaches out to touch me when I pass by.

Watching him "check out" is like an amputation. A tearing away. Then he smiles. His smile takes off in his pale blue eyes . . . crinkles his entire face . . . and lands in my heart. His smile is God's gift to me. It wraps a golden halo around my season of sadness.

I am so blessed to receive the special gifts God scatters throughout my dailiness.

And I know my season of joy will come again . . . when my husband enfolds me with an eager hug . . . on a street of gold in heaven.

I hadn't a clue that what was going on in Nancy's life was this serious. Or that she had such a way with words. I didn't know her husband, Lynn, and hadn't heard about their life together.

I'm not sure what I was writing—probably that stuff about the "glittering aspens." I was writing about scenery and how I, ever the subject of the sentence, was fitting in; she was dealing with impending death.

Sitting there in the big bed in our room trying to keep my feet warm, I couldn't get away from her words *scream* and *amputation*, which I never expected to hear from her. She had such a buoyancy and brightness about her that I didn't really know what to do with such edgy language. Looking back, those words were the first sign of the depth of emotion and experience she was carrying around inside. Yet even then, even in that poignant description of her "stern and splendid mate," words of hope far outweighed the sadness.

I never anticipated a time in my life when I would have—or want—a designated passenger. Particularly a little old lady. But after Colorado, after we found that we got along and could both keep a clean sink, some deeply hidden wanderlust took over, connecting us like Lewis and Clark.

One late-summer day I invited Nancy to join me on a trip to the mountains outside of Fresno to pick up my grown daughter, Molly, at camp. We'd been casual friends for a couple of years since rooming together, but on this trip, 350 miles up and back with a couple of nights in between, I began getting to know this person who had so fortuitously dropped into my life.

I was the driver; Nancy, the supply sergeant. (She lifted "snacks" to the sublime—Gouda and crackers, raisins and shelled pecans, bottled water, and always a smidge of dark chocolate.) Comparing notes, we quickly agreed that we loved car trips, anytime, anywhere.

The drive from San Diego to our destination took us up Interstate 5, through the snarl that is Los Angeles traffic, over the "Grapevine," where they warn you to turn off your air conditioning in the summer and where fog can overtake you in the winter. Then we merged onto the 99, a four-lane highway crowded with produce trucks and banked by scruffy fields. Dust devils swirled up from nowhere and elevated our bottled water to champagne status. We stopped in Bakersfield for lunch, splitting a salad and a tuna sandwich so thick we had to scoop out a good portion of the tuna to get it into our mouths.

North of Tulare I pulled out Molly's directions, a shortcut she guaranteed would cut off significant miles. But after several turns we found ourselves in orange groves and dirt roads with no shortcut in sight. Nancy's sense of adventure was high, though I was looking over my shoulder for either danger or assistance; I wasn't sure which. We finally spotted a fruit stand. As best as I could understand the Spanish directions, we needed to head *that* way, and off we went.

As we started up the mountain, every turn in the road offered an eyeful of greatness—boulders as big as bedrooms, granite and limestone cliffs, sugar pines with cones the size of footballs sharing the hillsides with cedars and stately sequoias. Nancy appreciated every bit of beauty as much as I'd hoped she would. Yes, indeed, we were suited to each other.

The camp sat between the mountains like the cone floor in a volcano. A walking trail encircled the lake, and canoes and paddleboats lined the narrow dock. I took the trail gleefully when we got there, while Nancy read in the car. She was chilly when I returned; I shed layers like a cross-country runner.

We had dinner in the lodge overlooking the lake, the water smooth like a glass floor you could slide on in your socks. The mountains, reflected perfectly in the water, seemed close enough to walk to and scale in one day, though they were miles away and out of our league.

Over dinner Nancy pulled a sheaf of papers from her black bag and began to read to me some of the vignettes she'd written and saved over the years. True stories about her encounters with the famous and not so famous. Some of them were sweet and saccharine, some were slightly scandalous, others were heart wrenching.

Words were tiny miracles to her. "I can't *not* write," Nancy used to say when asked about the craft. Her Uncle Harley was a printer. He published her first book, *Fluffy*, a tiny little chapter book she wrote when she was nine about the chicks she raised in their hotel bathtub and the prize-winning rooster that came from that brood.

About her beginnings as a writer, she once wrote:

As a child I remember looking under our Christmas tree for my stack of foolscap and a whole box of #2 lead pencils. They were always there, unwrapped.

what an old friend taught me about life

I got a diary once, but it didn't have enough room to hold all my words, and besides, foolscap was so comfortable.

My uncle was a printer, and I was raised among words. One of my favorite pastimes was to sit on a high stool in his print shop and watch him work. I vividly remember the day I decided to help, so I moved all the type around while he was occupied with a sluggish printing press. When he realized what I had done, he made me sit there through the long night correcting and editing the changes I had made. That night words became a way of life with me, and until I married I helped him edit his assignments.

Words and all their glory began to wind around us that night. Over dessert we shared favorite book titles, discovered our common love for finding precisely the right word, and began bickering over adverbs.

That weekend we had reservations to share a room at a little place nearby owned by some writer friends. They promised us an elaborate breakfast in front of the fireplace—because it's cool there in the mornings, even in August—then led us upstairs to a cozy room with a treetop view.

Our first night there Nancy took out her teeth.

She looked her age. Years of sun and sea had weathered her skin, and osteoporosis had bent her over like a tire jack. She'd begun to shuffle when I met her in her early seventies. She wasn't vain, but she took a quiet pride in her appearance—she liked her clothes to match and wore a lot of jersey, scheduled regular manicures, and usually wore earrings. But she cut her own hair and bobby pinned a little curl in the back to cover a thin spot. Her teeth were a little off kilter and filled in with bridges, which I wouldn't have noticed for a long time had she not taken them out that night at the B&B.

How people were drawn to her! She had a sort of instinctive, impetuous friendliness that intrigued you on the one hand and took the pressure off you on the other. She could start and build a relationship with anyone.

We spent the weekend walking trails and watching all the high-school kids who swarmed the camp. Nancy struck up conversations wher-

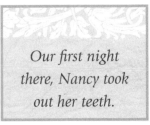

Our first night there, Nancy took out her teeth.

ever we were and seemed truly delighted to be in the presence of teenagers. Even the band, with Molly as the lone girl singer, captivated her, though the volume was so high we couldn't understand the words. "It's OK," she said. "I don't care. Aren't they wonderful?"

With Molly in the backseat, we left the mountains after a couple of days, left the solitude of no TV, no phones, no news. We were already establishing a congenial rhythm, a familiarity we both appreciated. It's always nice to find a friend in whose presence you're at ease. I would not have believed how comfortable I could feel with a little old lady.

at the mercy of clumsy souls

Nancy loved me and had a plan for my life that was birthed way back at our Colorado conference. She finally told me about it—she had wanted to turn me over her knee (her very words) that weekend for expressing my insecurities and fears about writing and about life in general. In fact, I realized later that she had been biting her tongue all weekend to keep from confronting me.

She didn't bite it for long.

She said she was surprised to see me "bending toward negativity" and had wracked her brain to think of encouraging ways to get me back on track. She had thought I was decisive, forward thinking, and courageous. I got us to Colorado in the first place and broke the inevitable deadlocks that arise when four very different, very nice women have to make decisions. But in Colorado she also saw my anxious side.

It soon became quite clear that Nancy and I came at life from very different points of view. It would prove to be our biggest point of contention and the fodder for the first major lesson she felt I needed to learn: *keep a positive attitude*.

We had a spirited discussion one sunny day, driving from

another writers' conference back to town, about first reactions, instinct, natural inclinations, and personality distinctions.

"Tell me what you see," I said, "that makes you think I'm such a negative person."

She shrugged a bit, propping her hand under her chin as if trying to contain what was about to come out of her mouth. Then she started in.

"You try too hard to cover every angle of what we're doing."

"What do you mean?"

"Oh, you know . . . 'now if we do this, we need to make sure we take care of this first'—that kind of stuff, like you're anticipating a problem."

"I'm thorough."

"So am I. I just don't worry about it or talk about it all the time. It takes all the fun away."

She had been biting her tongue all weekend to keep from confronting me. She didn't bite it for long.

I looked ahead, focusing on driving while I stewed on that a bit.

"Annnnd," she started again, ready for the final thrust, "I don't see how you can believe in God the way you say you do and be so worried about everything. You approach life with a frown on your face!"

I was still trying to process all this, very aware of the frown on my face, when she said lightly as we crested a hill, "But I'm not trying to analyze you. That's just how you are."

13

"You don't analyze me, but you call me on it."

"But I don't hold it against you."

That's true, she didn't, and I appreciated it. My negative first reactions, the glass-is-half-empty way I tend to look at life, the fear that rules me at times, were issues we talked about regularly. And in the middle of our conversation that day another illustration presented itself. Tooling along in my newly washed car, we came upon a shiny red, spanking-clean, double-bedded truck kicking up dirt as it sped along. As we passed it, at exactly the same moment, Nancy said, "Oh, what a beautiful red truck!" and I said, "I hope it doesn't get my car dirty."

> *Nancy was an indefatigable optimist. You could see it in the way she walked, sort of thrust forward and determined-like.*

Behold, a pattern emerged. The afternoon before, our instructor had given us a writing assignment. He told the beginning of a story and sent us off to finish it up on paper. This would produce no grades, would not be used for or against us in any way, would not reflect on our worth as people or our ability as writers. For all we knew, it might not even be seen by anyone else. It was merely an exercise. After he outlined our assignment, he said, "Write this on your paper: have fun." I did just as he said, wrote "have fun" on my paper, but absent-mindedly added a question mark. I glanced over at Nancy's papers as she gathered them together. She, of course, had written "have fun" with a smiley face and a big, fat exclamation point.

So I asked Nancy after we passed the truck, "What if it's *not* your natural inclination to think positively, to let things go? What if negativity is so immediate, it feels like instinct?" I wanted to defend myself, give credence to my melancholy temperament. Hold on to the notion that it's part of who I am and therefore all right.

I didn't get a satisfactory answer that afternoon, and we began a discussion that lasted in various forms the rest of her life. I did tell her that I don't believe it's my negative first thoughts that derail me but the fact that I don't move more quickly to upbeat ones. But she didn't buy it. She was convinced I could train myself so that my first thoughts *would* be positive ones.

I'm sure my brow was furrowed as I listened to her and contemplated such a sea change.

Nancy was an indefatigable optimist. You could see it in the way she walked, sort of thrust forward and determined-like, ready for a change of plan. She wasn't a frowner or a complainer, and it's what she most disliked in me. She reveled in the present and couldn't wait for the future. I'm fine with the present as long as I've had my coffee. The thought of the future can paralyze me.

She teased me with the promise that by the time we finished writing our book, her influence would be so strong, I'd be too laid back to get out of bed in the morning. I countered with my own expectation that she'd be so introspective she'd be neurotic. By the time she died, in some measure both predictions had come true.

I got a little defensive at times in the face of all that positive thinking she trumpeted around. One day in her little kitchen I asked her, "What if I can't help being a certain way? What if my attitudes are just . . . me?"

She gave me a look both incredulous and pitying.

I went on. "It could be heredity . . . or birth order . . . or environment. Lots of things factor into how we react to things and how we think."

"But you do have a choice," she countered. "*As a man thinks in his heart, so is he.*" That was one of her favorite Bible verses, and her friends heard it a lot.

I wasn't satisfied with such an easy answer, though, biblical or not. "I still think attitudes are shaped by many things," I said. "Maybe that whole list."

But I couldn't sway her at all. She even labeled me a pessimist, which really annoyed me because I knew that one word, that one expectation, didn't describe me completely.

It seemed she believed that attitudes should be as easy to mold as soft clay, with a little help from God. She wanted me to get with the program. But minds are not always so pliable, I wanted to argue. Not so flexible. Temperaments do shape us, and attitudes are at the mercy of clumsy souls who are all thumbs.

The more we talked, though, the more I was compelled to examine my own heart. I knew I wasn't living a defeated Christian life, moping around the house waiting for the other shoe to drop.

But just the possibility of certain events really made me anxious, and I couldn't justify that anymore. Can a negative attitude even survive in a heart of faith?

Faith is a mystery to me. On the one hand, it should be so simple: read the Bible so you know all about God, and then believe that He is who He says He is and that He will do what He says He will do.

On the other hand, there's that "leaping" stuff, that flinging yourself and your assumptions out over the precipice on the promise that there's an unseen hand, or wing, that will bear you up and out of danger. Like Indiana Jones and the chasm he steps into, finding an invisible but material pathway through the air.

The earliest hours of the mornings are the hardest for me. I've heard some say that those are the most creative moments in our lives, when we're sort of half asleep and ideas come and go so quickly. But my ideas bring me stress! I'm forever running down the list of all I have to do, and in the middle of the list, somehow, come thoughts like, *What if Ron dies in the next few years? Will I be able to handle it? Is he even going to wake up this morning?*

And then I reach over and nudge him just a little to make sure he will.

So, you ask, if you have this relationship with God that is supposed to provide all you need, why do you wrestle with it? My answer? I'm not so sure. But in the middle of all this angst about my angst, I know two things: God created me with my own little idiosyncrasies and personality. In fact, maybe He designed me in such a way as to keep me desperate for Him. I love that. But I also know that His loving heart wants my rapidly beating heart to be at peace.

Somewhere there has to be a place where I can live with Nancy's optimism, my personality, and God's blessing.

"Are you sure you're not in denial?" I asked Nancy once.

She denied denial. "I don't want to spend the time to analyze myself because I feel secure with who I am. I'm not that concerned about analyzing my psyche to find out if I've denied it or not!

"The good Lord gave me a grand outlook on life," she explained to me that day. "I'm able to let negative stuff go and hang on to positive thoughts. I don't analyze situations like you do."

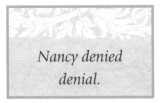

Nancy denied denial.

She went on to tell me about all the women she'd counseled—one-on-one, in small church groups, in a holding cell for newly convicted female criminals, even as a Welcome Wagon lady. After hearing so many women "wallow in the past, think negative thoughts in the present, and face the future with fear and trembling," she decided what kind of a person she wanted to be. ·

"God has given all of us a choice in how we deal with our lives," she said, "and I chose long ago to count my blessings. No matter how dismal the moment in time, there are always blessings. My natural instinct is 'Yes! Let's! I want to!'

"I love the idea," she said, "that we get up in the morning and look in the mirror and see the reflection of our attitudes. Our choice for that day is right there in the mirror."

"But," I urged her, "are you sure you're not repressing something? Are you sure there's not something deep inside you're not even aware of?"

I pressed it because she was unfolding her life to me, story after story, and despite her clever telling, her natural optimism, and her determination to shine a positive light on things, I couldn't imagine there was no grief or damage there. And maybe, just maybe, I was looking for a little ammunition.

where we came from
—nancy's story

Nancy had the most childlike heart and spirit of anyone I know well enough to make such observations about. I promise you, she was nineteen inside. Before I knew her well, I might have thought that her life had been a full and happy one, devoid of extreme pain or disillusionment. Wrong.

She was an only child, born in New York when Babe Ruth was a Yankee, Calvin Coolidge sat in the White House, and Charles Lindbergh was getting ready for his transatlantic flight. Her mother died of cancer when Nancy was four, and the images around that time were indelibly etched in her mind as her first childhood memories.

Most of the faces that weave across my memory screen from that day are vague shadows without names. But the faces of the two men wearing white coats, carrying my mother on a narrow white bed between them, are branded on my brain. I watched from the staircase, but the doctor shooed me away. "Nancy Lee, go upstairs to your room and shut the door!" I did what he told me and went up to my room trying not to cry. My black patent-leather shoes were beside my bed, and they made me feel good, so I put them on and went back to the staircase.

I hated that doctor—he always made my mother scream when he gave her a shot. The grownups never let me get near her. They said she hurt when I touched her and she should not be bothered. But whenever they left her alone, I'd sneak into her room. We'd hug each other, and I'd pat her hair. She liked that, and she never once said that it hurt her to hug me.

After Nancy's mother died, her father, a traveling salesman, gave her up to her aunt and uncle to rear. That's two "abandonments" right there, if you're counting. In her uncle, Nancy found a father, a loving protector who knew how to intrigue and cherish little girls. She called him Daddy from the start. But her aunt was a cool woman with no clue as to how to raise a child. Nancy couldn't call her Mother, but she gave her the name

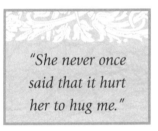

"*She never once said that it hurt her to hug me.*"

Ferdy after *Ferdinand the Bull* (her favorite children's book about a flower-loving bull), because Ferdy, like the bull, often held a flower to her nose.

She told me about the many days she spent as a six-year-old in the summer of 1930 playing up and down New York City's Fifth Avenue while Ferdy luxuriated in the Elizabeth Arden Salon. It sounded fascinating and adventurous until she clarified that her aunt *left her outside for hours* while she had her "treatments." New York City was a different place back then.

"What are you doing in there?" she asked Ferdy one day. "*Everything,*" Ferdy gushed, refusing to satisfy her curiosity.

Unfazed and trusting, Nancy would amuse herself by having animated but one-sided conversations with the doorman and skipping along beside the neighborhood policeman as he walked his beat. Ferdy took Nancy with her regularly and, when she got a little older, allowed her to visit the F.A.O. Schwarz toy store a few blocks away. Her imagination was nurtured there.

She spent her childhood living in New York hotels and in the company of adults, often tucked in a corner under the piano during their cocktail parties or behind a blanket fort having tea parties with her dolls. She considered dolls her peers and found it easy to drift in and out of make-believe scenes from her favorite books. In the midst of all that solitude, she claimed she always felt secure, happy, and loved.

Not until she was in her forties did she fully recall her mother's death and her father's desertion and grasp that the people she considered her parents were actually her aunt and uncle. No one had bothered to clear it up for her in all those years.

I couldn't help but play the armchair psychologist after hearing that story. What kind of mark is left by such a realization and such abandonments (intentional or not) on the psyche of a little girl? I wondered how it was that Nancy seemed so free of sorrow, free of the need to blame, free to love others so easily.

Who was this woman riding in my car? And could we, who came at life from such different places, ever really relate?

Nancy married her first husband at Christmastime during the height of World War II. Picture young men in uniform swarming Fifth Avenue, frantic to buy gifts before the stores close; New York City resplendent with twinkling lights, silently falling snowflakes, Salvation Army Santas ringing their bells, and ice skaters lining up at Rockefeller Center.

"I carried my ice blue wedding dress from an exclusive little shop to the Biltmore Hotel," she wrote. "Rushing through the revolving door, warm air wrapped around me. Canaries sang in their cages in the hallways, and I met my future father-in-law for the first time. Gray hair framed his tan face, and his calculating blue eyes swept over me from head to toe. He skipped the formality of a friendly greeting and honed in on his mission.

"'You have nice broad hips,' he said. 'It should be a cinch for you to have babies. I'll give you a thousand dollars if you have a baby within a year. Two thousand if it's a boy!'"

She went for it, and Johnny was born within the year. Kathy followed four years later.

Nancy and her father-in-law were friends for fifty years, more than twice as long as her marriage lasted. For, after only three weeks of married life, Nancy knew she'd made a huge mistake. Her new husband, as she described him, "was one of those charming men with great potential who couldn't handle alcohol and wouldn't choose to stop drinking."

But she stuck with him, believing in honoring her marriage vows. Finally, after twenty-three years, their marriage ended when late one night, in their Southern California community, Nancy's husband left the house drunk with a revoked driver's license. She found him at a bar and did her best to get his keys and take his car, but he overpowered her, shoved her out onto the pavement, and sped away.

"I lay there looking up at the stars and felt God reach down and touch my cheek. 'It's OK,' He seemed to say. 'You can leave him now.' My girlfriend who had come with me knelt beside me and stroked my hair. The garbage cans smelled awful. My left hand rested in a puddle of oil, filling my wedding ring with yucky stuff. The stale odor of liquor and cigars drifted out from the open back door of the bar. Harsh music blasted the night, followed by laughter and cursing. Glasses clinked and my marriage dissolved into the asphalt."

After her divorce, and with her children grown and gone, Nancy sold her beautiful home in Southern California. At the urging of friends, she moved aboard their old powerboat in Long Beach Harbor to see if she liked living on the water. The boat leaked badly, and she had to sleep with her hand dangling on the cabin floor—when her fingers got wet, it was time to pump. There were no bathroom facilities, no heat of any kind, and no cooking accommodations. She lived mostly on raisins, dates, and walnuts (the origin of our travel snacks?) and loved every minute of it.

When she convinced her friends that she was serious, they helped her find a sturdy old boat that she bought, moved aboard, gutted, and fixed up in luxurious fashion. Those were some of the happiest days of her life, she told me, the days she climbed over timbers, spackled dents, wallpapered abused bulkheads, and painted and varnished to make a home.

She named her boat *Tough Optimist* and the dinghy *T.O. Too*, because of a book she had read that depicted the kind of mental attitude she had decided to adopt.

At the marina she met a guy who lived in a nearby slip who taught her to sail, taking her out early in the morning to practice maneuvers and teaching her to navigate without sideswiping her neighbors. Joe ultimately became the escape from her old life. Joe and Nancy sailed off to Costa Rica, where they bought 350 acres of prime beach property, creating a unique and off-the-beaten-path oasis for other sailors. It was a huge undertaking, as everything they needed entailed rowing across the bay.

As chief cook and bottlewasher and a whole lot more, Nancy did everything from cleaning toilets to playing bridge with traveling yachtsmen. She made beds in the dirt-floored, screened cabins, cooked at midnight, and served by

"Harsh music blasted the night. Glasses clinked and my marriage dissolved into the asphalt."

kerosene lanterns (no electricity, no generator), and even laid a thousand-foot cement-and-flagstone sidewalk all by herself. At fifty.

Nancy lived with Joe for seven years in Costa Rica. He proved to be the first love interest in her life who treated her with respect and on whom she could depend, though she spoke about him sparingly, not trying to justify her actions but keeping their relationship to herself. Joe remained her faithful friend—but not her true love—until the day she died.

Nancy had to have been the most incurable romantic I've ever known, especially if you take into consideration her history. Her early models of marriage left much to be desired; she had a difficult first marriage of her own and never did feel compelled to marry Joe; she watched her children's relationships waver for a while; and yet she continued to hold on to her belief that a man and woman could live happily ever after, just like in fairy tales. Maybe because it really did happen to her—finally.

Looking up from that cement-and-flagstone walk one morning, she watched a yacht sail in carrying a couple from Arizona, Lynn and Olive Bayless. She concluded Lynn was an amateur when it took him three tries to set his anchor, but it turned out he was a master sailor with plenty of nautical miles under his belt. She pitched in, helping him and his wife of forty-two years take care of the necessities sailors in port need to attend to.

Their little resort community was shocked a few days later when

Olive died in a freak accident with no apparent explanation. Apart from the obvious trauma of a sudden suspicious death, dying in a tropical foreign country brought its own set of problems. Nancy did her best to help Lynn through the hardest time of his life by walking him through all the complications required to lay his wife to rest.

Lynn was an impulsive man, and this was her first indication: after Olive's death he left his boat with her and Joe and flew home to Phoenix, intending to stay for several months, but returning in nine days . . . for her! I don't know if you could call it love at first sight, but they certainly didn't take much time for getting to know each other or for established conventions of mourning. Or for letting Joe down easily.

"Lynn took my hand and never let it go," she told me. "He was an extremely impetuous man. He had an adventurous spirit and a commanding presence. Just what I needed." He took her away on his boat like a pirate making off with the sea captain's daughter, and she never looked back.

They were married, in characteristically dramatic fashion, in an Arizona jail, where Lynn's friend, the chaplain, performed the ceremony.

On our wedding day I wore a new yellow suit, and Lynn put on a bolo in lieu of a tie. Wind swept across the desert and ruffled my freshly curled hair when we stopped for a corsage of yellow roses.

The jail was nestled in the middle of the mountainous desert with nothing near it for miles. The total isolation appealed to us, and the tiny chapel gleamed with fresh paint and warm radiators. Our minister had chosen his wife and a staff member to be our witnesses, and two of the inmates were our congregation.

No strains of "Here Comes the Bride," silver vases of white lilies, or flickering candles in entwined candelabras graced our surroundings, but we felt God smile down at us. The wind howled and blew forty knots to rattle the window-panes. It seemed fitting weather for two sailors to become one, even in the desert.

Nancy rarely spoke of that transitional episode in her life—of the quaint, tiny cabins she and Joe built on their land overlooking the Gulf of Nicoya, of their affair and how it became a lifelong friendship, of how she so suddenly took up with another man.

Jennie, Vicki, and I asked plenty of blunt questions and even enlisted her daughter, Kathy, to fill in a few of the blanks. Nancy's quick decisions about Joe and Lynn were a shock to her children. "After all," Kathy recalled, "all we knew was that this man's wife suddenly died, and now my mom was leaving Joe and sailing off around the world with him." The unspoken questions were, is she safe and is she crazy?

But it wasn't long before everyone could see how happy Lynn made her and how wonderfully suited they were to each other. Kathy and Johnny not only recognized Lynn as a man of character and integrity, but they also allowed him to fill the father role in their lives. Joe must have accepted it too, because interestingly enough, he remained friends with Nancy *and* Lynn, showing up to visit in San Diego now and then for the rest of their lives.

Lynn was an adventurer, and Nancy was ready for anything. He would catch her eye, crook his finger to beckon her, and say, "We're off in thirty minutes. Better yet, thirty seconds." If he had a toothbrush sticking out of his shirt pocket, it meant "pack a bag, we're going on a trip." She wouldn't really know what he had in mind, but she'd be ready and off they'd go, by land or sea or air.

In 1977, when Nancy was fifty-three and Lynn sixty-eight, they embarked on the expedition of a lifetime, crossing the Atlantic from Spain's Canary Islands to the West Indies in a thirty-foot sailboat. By themselves.

We were adventurers! We had sold almost everything we owned and gotten our lives down to a duffel bag apiece. We had a sturdy little new boat right from the factory in England. We were senior citizens, but healthy, knowledgeable, and young at heart. God was in control so there was nothing to fear.

The tiny island of Hierro seemed to melt into the horizon behind us, leaving over three thousand miles of the shining Atlantic Ocean stretched out before us, like a humongous roll of aluminum foil.

The world of our crossing teemed with life and glory. The flying fish soared about like Piper Cubs on Sunday afternoon. Every night several crashed on our deck and stuck like glue. Porpoise tumbled about like toddlers at a birthday party. Their inquisitive, smiling faces checked us out as they leaped over one another with total abandon. They often came in groups of three and loved to race, crossing inches ahead of our bow. One glorious day as I was washing my hair, twenty-seven of them frolicked around me, jumping higher than my head.

> *"'What are you doing to yourself out there?' One word popped into my mind and out of my mouth. 'Everything!'"*

The weather changed outfits with alarming and breathtaking rapidity. Short-lived squalls tore across the ocean like racing ice skaters by day and in phosphorescent chorus lines at night. Sometimes they hit with such sudden force, I'd stand on the instrument panel and reach up through the sliding-glass hatch to hold on to Lynn's ankles while he stood outside on the cabin top and reefed the mainsail. I silently prayed for God to hold on to him too. And He did.

I used my Atlantic Laundromat almost every day, hanging on for dear life as I reached for clothes and pins. Wet towels flapped in my face, while the sea unrolled behind me like huge bolts of carpet.

At sea, fresh water became our main concern. We never had enough. I finally succumbed to bathing with salt water and discovered the world's most exhilarating way to cleanliness.

My preparation started with two large plastic pails and one small one. The small one had a lanyard attached to it, and this enabled me to lean over the side of the boat, while we were under way, and scoop up seawater. I hauled it aboard until I had filled the two large pails.

I set out all the necessary tools to give myself complete beauty-salon gratification and took off my grubbies. I shampooed my hair, combed out the tangles, and brush-curled it dry by facing into the wind. Next, I scrubbed my whole body with shampoo until my skin squeaked with cleanliness. I rinsed off with a bucket of salt water and drip-dried or rubbed my skin briskly with my towel, depending on the temperature of the day.

Next, I squeezed out a handful of avocado body lotion and smoothed it over my skin. Then I put a dab of perfume behind my ears and on my wrists. I clipped, cut, and filed my nails, but only polished my toenails, because fingernail polish chips almost immediately while doing chores aboard.

My cockpit cosmetology could last for hours. One day my husband stuck his head out of the hatch and asked, "What are you doing to yourself out there?"

Grinning, one word popped into my mind and out of my mouth. "Everything!"

I finally knew why Ferdy adored Elizabeth Arden's

Salon. I could appreciate her need to be alone. And I emulated her satisfied, smiling expression as I wiggled into a clean T-shirt and hung my towel over the tiller to dry.

After forty days at sea we approached our destination, English Harbor on the island of Antigua in the West Indies.

Lynn came up to the wheelhouse from below, where he had been checking and rechecking my navigation. "Well, dear," he said, "if your figures are correct, we should look out and see land!"

We looked to port and saw only a sloppy, gray day. Then we looked to starboard and, sure enough, we saw the dim formation of an island! We jumped up and down, hugging each other. Thank You, Lord! Thank You, Lord! Thank You, Lord! The words kept spinning through my mind.

Lynn made coffee and brought me a steaming cup laced with cocoa and cradled my face in his strong hands. "You OK?"

"I'm OK."

"Good. I'm going to take a nap."

While he slept, I watched Antigua loom larger and larger on the horizon. I could see spray crashing against her reefs. Tomorrow we'll have ice cream and crisp carrots. We'll see buses, taxis, and planes. We'll lose touch with our reality out here.

Suddenly I didn't want our forty-day voyage to end. Where is home? It's right here . . . where my heart is. I wasn't prepared for traffic, exhaust fumes, and masses of humanity.

Then I thought about mail call. A thick, juicy hamburger. Hershey's with almonds. A real telephone. Letters from home.

I looked back at the vast expanse of the Atlantic Ocean, just as Lynn got up from his nap. My eyes caught and held his eyes. A wave of exaltation passed between us. We did it! We lived through the nightmarish dream of so many sailors. We survived the rigors of wind and sea. We did it in our thirty-foot sailboat, and with our Lord's continuous, miraculous blessings.

where we came from
—my story

I'm the first of three girls from a family heavy on integrity but not too clued in to spiritual things. Harry Truman was president the year I was born. William Faulkner won the Nobel Prize in literature, and Spencer Tracy and Katharine Hepburn starred together in *Adam's Rib*.

I grew up in Denver in houses with lawns that my dad groomed with a rattling hand-pushed mower, producing exactly the sound that Ray Bradbury said should usher in the New Year. "Who was the fool who made January first New Year's Day?" Bradbury wrote in *Dandelion Wine*. "No, they should set a man to watch the grasses across a million . . . lawns, and on that morning when it was long enough for cutting . . . there should be a great swelling symphony of lawn mowers . . ."

When I think of my Denver home I think of that sound, and the cooing mourning doves, and the sweet smell of cut grass. Funny, it's not the winters that come immediately to mind, but the summers. I think of lying in my bed at night, the cool breeze mixing the smells of suntan oil and chlorine, my skin tight with sunburn from a day of swimming and "laying out," blissfully ignorant of the spots that would magically appear on my legs thirty years later from all that exposure.

My mom was easygoing, kind, witty, gentle, Southern born with the trace of an accent only when she talked with her Tennessee relatives. She planted white petunias in the big planter in the middle of our back patio; strung fat colored lights around the porch for summer dinner parties; had a way with shrimp Creole, fried chicken, and rice and gravy; played "Stardust Memories" on our old upright piano; walked the neighborhood for the March of Dimes, and helped exercise a neighbor's disabled child. She took care of Koko and Wags, our Shetland sheepdogs, even though we'd promised to do it ourselves, and she let us name the cat Kitty-Boo, which is a motherly act if ever there was one. She was the first one to apologize after disagreements, though I can't think of one that was her fault, and she scratched our backs late into the night. And like most moms she went through a couple of very peculiar hairstyles.

In retrospect she was a woman of quiet faith, unflinching integrity, and immeasurable grace. She was *not* the energy in our family, keeping the enthusiasm high all the time; she was the lifeblood, the breath, the peace. She died of cancer in 1990, when I was forty, too young to lose my mother. I miss her all the time.

When I think of Daddy, I picture him in his white dress shirt with the collar open and sleeves rolled up, khaki pants, and clean white tennis shoes. He's sitting in the green chair, holding his pipe gently in his teeth, grinning, peering at his three daughters over his tortoise-shell reading glasses and the daily paper.

He was an entrepreneur/businessman who adored us and we him. He believed in us, respected us, and swooned with admiration when we walked down the stairs all decked out for some special occasion. We danced on his feet while he hummed Mills Brothers songs, out of tune, in our ears and looked forward to Christmas Eve when he would gather us all on the couch and tell us his version of *A Christmas Carol*, complete with all the scary voices.

But he was also subject to depression, and that, combined with his unpredictable temper (though it was rarely directed at us) and later his business problems, affected our little-girl lives in ways my two sisters and I are still trying to pinpoint.

> *Though he was wrong, my father died a hero. It makes a difference.*

My father died in 1983 of a self-inflicted gunshot wound. My sister tried to get hold of us in California, but we'd taken the phone off the hook. Somehow she was able to track down a co-worker who knocked on our door at 10:00 p.m. and told us to call home. I screamed into the phone when she told me, shaken . . . but not really surprised. Daddy had struggled for years to provide for us in what he considered a fitting manner, and when business got tough and money scarce he saw it as a personal failure—regardless of anything we might say.

36

Though his death seems like it should have created deep-seated torment, it was softened by our age, by our frequent expressions of love to and from him, and by our realization that he saw his action as heroic, as the one thing he could do to relieve our mom of the stress she'd been under. In his eyes he gave his life for her; from notes we know that was his motivation.

Though he was wrong, my father died a hero. It makes a difference.

Of course, the way he handled his life had an impact. My sister reminded me recently of how rocky Sunday nights were, the night before the workweek began again with all its uncertainties. His life and death and who knows how many other influences have planted in me control issues and a tendency both to perfectionism and an avoidance of powerful emotions. And tucked inside all that fussiness is a kernel of fear and insecurity.

Put fear and insecurity together with control and just a smattering of gregariousness, and you get an anxious woman who talks about it. I'm thinking it's not a very attractive personality trait. Nancy didn't like it in me, either.

I left Denver for college in Oregon, graduated with a music-education major, and landed a good teaching job in an elementary school in a district that valued the arts. Luckily, I also graduated with a good husband, Ron, which was particularly fortunate as I realized quickly that teaching wasn't my gift. While I'd been in college he had started seminary. On the side, in between theology classes and homework, he sold vacuum cleaners, until one night he found himself convincing a poor family with no rugs or carpet that they needed a $295 Filter Queen. That was the end of that, and he took an associate pastor's position in a little church close to home.

A couple of years later life took an unexpected turn as a result of a little daydreaming. Ron had to come up with a research topic for his doctoral thesis. He'd asked me to do the driving for the two hours from his parents' home in Bremerton, Washington, to our tiny one-bedroom, low-income apartment in Portland. He'd reclined his seat and, in the quiet darkness, the calm of night traveling, he came up with an interesting proposition.

"What would you say," he began, feeling out my mood, "if we decided to take a trip across the country to get material on what the church is doing in discipleship? I could write it up for my thesis."

"And . . . ," I prompted, my eyes on the road.

"And we'd somehow get a motor home and ask another couple to go with us . . . and it could take up to nine months."

No way, I thought. "Tell me more," I said.

"Well, we could make appointments beforehand to meet with pastors and Christian leaders around the country for interviews. We'd have to quit our jobs"—my interest was piqued now—"and find the money somewhere."

I really thought it was just speculation, simply Ron thinking and dreaming aloud. Just one of those wild ideas that deserves discussion but doesn't amount to anything. But he took the idea to the president of the seminary he was attending and got the go-ahead, and not just the encouragement but also letters of introduction, the motor home, *and* a gas card, even though significant gas wars raged at the time.

It happened just like he dreamed it would. We took off in August of 1973 in a twenty-foot motor home for seven months . . . with another couple.

From the start, once we had enlisted Alan and Theda to travel with us, we prayed very specifically for the motor home. In fact, we had a ten-point prayer list. It would be close quarters for a very long time, and we young marrieds needed as much privacy as possible in that twenty feet. So we prayed for two queen-sized beds with one above the cab and one in the back, rather than on the side. (We hung a curtain across the middle of the "aisle.") We prayed for a great sound system for our eight-track tapes, for adequate kitchen facilities, for the shower in the bathroom . . . and even for that gas card. Every specific item on our list God provided.

Each morning we planned our route to correspond with the interviews we had scheduled and some of the sights we wanted to see. And we made it a point to stop at certain restaurants across the country a friend had detailed for us. We hit them all, though one time we were rejected because we were inappropriately dressed, and another time we were too late to a rural hole-in-the-wall with great catfish and hush puppies on the menu. We hunkered down in our little home and spent the night in the parking lot, showing up for Sunday brunch right on time the next morning.

It's a pretty amazing thing to have the time and reason to step away from jobs and home for such a trip. And it's even more amaz-

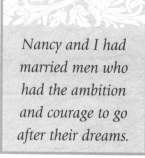

Nancy and I had married men who had the ambition and courage to go after their dreams.

ing to share the experience with another young couple. Yes, we met some great Christian leaders and visited thriving ministries. Yes, we collected enough data for Ron's thesis. But as you can imagine, the bigger "research" involved learning to live in twenty feet of space with people who weren't related to us.

This trip was pivotal in our lives because the connections we made set us up for five years of working in a church in Philadelphia, eight years with Campus Crusade's graduate school/seminary in Southern California, and finally moving Ron and me, with our two young children, to San Diego.

After all their adventures, Nancy and Lynn landed in San Diego as well, docking in the marina at Shelter Island. They lived on their little boat nearly twenty years, developing lifelong friendships with other boat people and folding themselves into a budding church where we finally met.

Nancy and I had married men who had the ambition and courage—and opportunity—to go after their dreams. And we'd gone along.

a giggle of women

When Nancy and I began to hang out, our husbands stayed home. Lynn encouraged her to get out now and then, and Ron's schedule was always full. Meanwhile, I continued to find myself somewhat incredulous that my new friend was a senior citizen. I had nothing against the idea; I just hadn't been looking for it.

Friends come easily enough at elementary school—when we're forced into a pairing because our last names begin with the same letter, or neither is (or both are) picked for the softball team. In high school and college, friends begin to define us. They help form our politics, determine our wardrobes, challenge our taste in music and dates, and influence our spiritual quests.

Young moms make friends through their children. You roll your child to the park, scoop him out of his stroller, and plop him gently in the sandbox next to another child. And so it begins. You swap life stories with his mom, and before you know it, your old friends become her new friends and vice versa.

But when your kids are grown, your nest is empty, and she and her family have moved to Chicago, where do you find new friends?

I will admit to a diminishing cache of girlfriends when my

kids grew up and moved out. It wasn't a lack of need, I suppose, but somehow when I didn't have to find a carpool or a playgroup, I didn't work at friendship quite so hard.

Then Nancy came along, helping to identify my need and meet it at the same time. Our children finally met . . . but not in the sandbox . . . and I was awfully glad to come across a new friend who could coax me into an occasional afternoon movie or a five-hundred-mile car trip.

Nancy once wrote of our travels, "I'm always glad to be tearing off into the morning sunrise with this young friend of my heart, not because I'm desperate for diversion but because I've always been ready to go . . . and I *love* car trips." We often compared notes about the almost visceral sensation (something we never really could put into words) that we felt whenever we were finally on the road.

With all the available ways to travel these days, car trips are still my favorite. Maybe it's the jeans and T-shirt attire or not having a to-the-minute departure time. Maybe it's because I can throw something I've forgotten to pack in the backseat at the last minute. Maybe it's an issue of control.

I remember just a few car trips with my family growing up. There was the one where we were driving from Denver to Southern California for spring break and got caught in a freak snowstorm over Wolf Creek Pass. A large truck inadvertently forced us

a giggle of women

off the road into a ditch, and the resulting exposure to the snow and cold as he got us moving again brought on a gout attack for my father. We detoured to the Grand Canyon and spent the week there, he with his swollen knee elevated in the room and Mom and we three girls peering through the fog at the nearly invisible canyon, shivering in the lightweight clothes we had packed for the beach. It wasn't very fun.

With all the available ways to travel these days, car trips are still my favorite.

The nighttimes were the best. Our station wagon would be overloaded, yet we always saved room for a trough between the luggage, and we lined it with blankets or a sleeping bag. One at a time we could lie there and look out the back window at the stars, which were ever so brilliant driving out of Denver, already a mile closer in distance. The long, empty roads in Wyoming or New Mexico and the white noise of the car somehow ushered in serious, satisfying conversations about dreams and desires. It was always a tossup—do I want to lie in the back looking at the stars or hunch over the front seat and get in on the stories?

Nancy could paint such a picture . . .

As a little girl I loved scrambling into the backseat of Daddy's car. Loved the leather smell and his pipe smoke drifting over me. Loved the vistas that seemed to whiz past us. Loved falling asleep and trying to guess where we were when I woke up. In almost eighty years nothing has changed for me. My face beams when I think of car trips.

When Mary first gave me a ride, I loved the smell of her Jeep and of her. These things matter. Mary is the perfect car-trip companion. She absorbs nature and is constantly aware of our surroundings. This virtue also makes her a good driver.

There are so many side effects to car trips, and we relish them all: the crackle of a AAA map as we open it and peer at the interstates; the challenge of trying to match the creases together before putting the map away; finding a squeaky-clean rest room at a gas station that has a freezer filled with frozen ice-cream bars by the cash register; the intrigue of opening a menu in a new restaurant; the pleasure of silence, of music, and of storytelling.

We are never bored. Car trips fill us with delight and anticipation.

Nancy's and my "Rules for the Road" were these: Don't rush things. Avoid fast food. Sleep in separate beds. Keep the sink clean. Take the scenic route. Head for the beach. Make the other's bed when she's not looking. Wash the windshield and pick up ice cream when you stop for gas.

One spring morning I gave Ron a peck on the check and tossed my pillow into the back of my Jeep Cherokee. The car was gassed and oiled, the tires filled, and freshly creased maps waited in the glove compartment. I drove to Nancy's condo and pulled into a space next to her green Dodge, "Peppermint." Yes, she named her cars. I wasn't late, but as usual she was standing on the walk already waiting, eager to get on the road to another conference with Jennie, Vicki, and me.

Her feet were surrounded by black bags—a "wheelie" with her clothes, a toiletries kit, a satchel filled with vitamins, and a bag with all the papers she wanted to read to me or work on herself, each one sealed carefully in a zipped plastic bag. She literally climbed into the front seat—she was about a head shorter than I, and it was a bit of a step up—and arranged the food so it was at our fingertips. I glimpsed green grapes that made my mouth water.

We settled into our separate spaces with smug contentment. Our tires made comforting, spinning tire sounds on the pavement, and once we had fought our way through traffic, brilliant green grasses smudged with yellow mustard flowers waved at us, encouraged by a gentle summer breeze. We left early enough to know we'd make it before dark, and that made the trip even more enjoyable.

"Could you grab me something to nibble on?" Mary asked. I reached into our stash behind the seats and came up with crunchy green grapes, crisp wheat crackers, and little balls of Gouda wrapped in red cellophane. I ripped the white strip off the cheese wrapper and handed her the soft, creamy ball. Her even white teeth (all her own, I'm sure) sank into it, and she sighed with appreciation.

She smiled at me and reached over to pat my gnarled hand.

I smiled back. My gums have receded, and the teeth on my partial bridge hang lower on the left side, but she doesn't care.

We met Jennie and Vicki at the conference center and found our adjoining rooms. Feeling adventurous, Nancy claimed the top bunk as soon as we walked in the door. She spread out her stash of chocolate, raisins, and pecans, and what was left of the grapes, on the lower bunk, tossed her writing satchel up onto the upper mattress, and began the climb up the ladder to claim her territory.

> *Together, Nancy and I made one dynamite woman— brave and vigilant, spontaneous and controlled, practical and eccentric.*

The other girls were stretched out on the double bed and I was unpacking when suddenly Nancy let out a little screech, and we looked over to see her halfway up the ladder . . . stuck. It had been perhaps ten years since she'd met the challenge of a top bunk and, though she didn't want to admit it, her ladder-climbing muscles were letting her down.

I grabbed her bottom half, thinking I should push her up. Vicki, suppressing a laugh because she didn't want to make Nancy laugh and lose her grip, began to pull her down. Jennie, as she generally does in emergencies, consoled her with tender loving words and took the catcher position, ready to cushion her fall. All the while Nancy clung precariously to the ladder with all her strength, afraid to budge and, I found out later, really frightened.

a giggle of women

Finally, Vicki cracked up and Nancy followed suit, and something had to give.

Somehow, very carefully, we ended up a giggle of women on the floor, with no serious injuries. That ignominious beginning set the stage for the entire conference. We were on the verge of out of control all weekend. And in the middle of the first night, I woke up to Nancy in hysterics under her covers trying to be quiet. She had herself so tied up in her nightgown that she'd given herself a "wedgie" and could not get untangled. She couldn't stop laughing. Me neither.

Together, Nancy and I made one dynamite woman—brave and vigilant, spontaneous and controlled, practical and eccentric. And though you might read those descriptions and think you can figure out to whom they belonged, who gets which label, you'd be wrong if you think our responses were always so cut-and-dried. Which was precisely my point.

Like at another conference in Colorado. In a valiant effort to unleash the creativity of the writers, musicians, artists, and poets of the group, the organizers of this conference gave us the opportunity to work in a medium outside our primary one. I chose clay, something in which I have absolutely no training and no experience beyond my Play-Doh days. It was a bold move for me, to try something new and risk embarrassment. Nancy, on the other hand, stuck with words. We didn't talk about her motives, but I wonder now if she was choosing a safe route, and if that was evidence that there were times she wanted very much to stay in her comfort zone.

I was really, really hoping that this experience would wake up that proverbial inner child people keep telling me I have, and that I would come out with something glorious and creative and surprising. But it didn't happen.

The clay lady gave us a lump of cool clay. "Work it," she said, and I was proud I knew what she meant. She continued, "Meditate on our scripture, Psalm 62:1–2, 'My soul finds rest in God alone. . . . He alone is my rock and my salvation.' Now let God work that verse out through your fingers into your clay. He will show you what to sculpt."

Yeah, right, I thought, but I went for it. I meditated with all my heart and emptied myself of all the extraneous thoughts I possibly could . . . and came up with no inspiration whatsoever.

So I took my lump back to our room after lunch. (I was the only one with homework.) Nancy was energetic, talkative, interested in what I was doing. As she watched me she got more and more tickled. I was perched on our wide, inviting window sill doing my very best to be creative and not say anything negative about the experience as I worked that lump. At one point the hint of a rabbit's haunches appeared in my clay. "Look," I said, calling her over. Unfortunately, I had to explain it, show her what I saw that she didn't, and it just set her to giggling again. It was sympathetic giggling, but it was giggling nonetheless.

I never did become the clay prodigy I'd hoped to become. But in the last few minutes of clay class a shape emerged—the cowed head and mantle of a monk, a servant of God, with his hands clasped under his robe (no way was I going to try hands) and the faint intimation of a face and beard. He sits on my bookshelf today. And you know what I remember when I see him? Nancy, and how much I made her laugh.

grace like rain

One day on the road we were talking, again, about the men in our lives. I pressed Nancy for more information on the Joe story. With a little shrug and a cryptic look in her eye, she said, "Things changed." That was an understatement.

And then she told me what else happened in her life at that time.

The summer just before she met Lynn, Nancy took a break from Costa Rica to manage a Florida beach resort. Shortly after she arrived, she hired an older woman as a housekeeper who mysteriously announced to Nancy right up front, "I think *you* are the reason for my being here." On her first lunch break she asked Nancy if she was a Christian, to which Nancy replied she'd always considered herself one. Then the woman asked if she was saved. Nancy wasn't sure how to answer that, and the housekeeper challenged her by saying, "If you were, you'd know it!"

The housekeeper convinced her to go to church with her that week, where Nancy burst into tears during communion.

The church was beautiful. The people were friendly, and I felt happy to be there. I was surprised, during communion, when I started to cry. I was unable to stop my tears, but I didn't feel embarrassed. The housekeeper put her arm around me as I sobbed through the closing hymn.

When I got control of myself, we joined some of the congregation gathered in a lovely room with chintz chair covers and softly lighted lamps. Delicious-smelling coffee and homemade cookies were being served, but I wasn't hungry. I chose a floor cushion and huddled against the housekeeper's chair.

I felt awful. Guilty. Unworthy. Hateful. I played with the carpet pile, and I hoped I wouldn't throw up.

> "I felt awful. Guilty. Unworthy. Hateful. I played with the carpet pile, and I hoped I wouldn't throw up."

The pastor came in and asked me to introduce myself. He said they really cared about me. I shrugged. He asked me if I had given my life to the Lord. I shook my head. He wondered if I knew how much Jesus loved me. I said I wasn't lovable.

The housekeeper stroked my hair, as though I were a child at her feet. Unexpectedly, words tumbled out of my mouth and spewed over the carpet. I admitted my faults, and I exposed my fears. I revealed things I had done that I knew were wrong and hurtful to God.

Nancy's heart had been softened toward God years before when she was a girl spending time with her beloved grandfather, a retired judge. When she visited him in Washington, DC, he took her on walks, showed her the stars, and splashed with her through rain puddles sprinkled with cherry blossoms. Perched on the footstool at his feet, she'd listen to him read his Bible and soak up his words. The judge was a kind, godly man who taught her about God's love and goodness. By the time he died when she was ten (*another* abandonment?), he had coached her in Scripture verses that she could recite like nursery rhymes.

One of those verses was, "Do all things without murmurings and disputings." Hmmm.

All this came back to her in Florida. She always said her grandfather gave her the world, that he introduced her to God. But it had taken her forty years to fully appreciate his message.

That night, in that little church, at the foot of her housekeeper's chair, she let go of years of living her own way. Grace like rain poured over her. It was a revolutionary encounter, which she capped off later by herself on the sugary beach under the stars, accepting God's forgiveness and the resulting peace and love.

Nancy knew she had a lot of stuff to work out in her life. First there was Joe. We were never quite sure if she left Joe because she felt guilty about living with him or because Lynn swept her off her feet. Or both. Then there was Lynn himself. He showed enough spiritual interest at the beginning to "get them to a chapel," but he didn't go to church regularly with her until later in his life.

Still, Nancy's belief in Jesus set the course for how she would live the twenty-some years of their marriage. As soon as they docked in San Diego she found a church—our church—and was there as much as possible, filling up on spiritual food. And in the end, Lynn was feasting as well.

Whereas you could say that Nancy came to faith in Christ because she recognized her need, I accepted Christ because it sounded like the right thing to do. I'm the firstborn, after all. Responsible.

Though I came of age in the turbulent sixties, I didn't burn my bra or get caught up in the drug scene, run off with a boy or suffer through significant hardship or pain. I had my own baggage, though, and by the time I got to college, I knew myself pretty well. I didn't like how moody I was, how easily swayed I could be, how weak my convictions were. (You'd have thought me a prime target for outside influences, but somehow along with my weakness was a timidity strong enough to protect me. Or maybe it was God . . .) So when this cute guy a year ahead of me in school explained the gospel to me, how I could begin a personal relationship with God, it seemed like the right thing to do. So I prayed with him . . . then I married him.

Though I made the transformation from moody college girl without spiritual sensitivity to moody college girl *with* spiritual sensitivity, I rarely experienced the deep emotions, the powerful feeling of love for God that other people talked about.

Occasionally I would hear an admonition to "return to your first love," meaning go back to that initial devotion you felt for

God. I understood the directive; I just couldn't comply. For some reason my emotions hadn't caught up with my beliefs. I wonder now if I was subconsciously suppressing *any* powerful feelings.

Then some years ago, after Nancy and I became friends and she began challenging me in a few areas, I decided something had

Oh my. It just hit me. Maybe my first thoughts are becoming positive ones!

to change. It wasn't that I believed God was disappointed in me or that I needed to change to be worthy of His attention. I just wasn't satisfied anymore to remain emotionally dry when it came to this precious relationship.

So I began praying earnestly for a passion for God. I'd be out on my morning walks and I would simply say, "Lord, give me a passion for You. I know You love me and I love You, but I want to *feel* it. I want to be overwhelmed with feeling for You. Give me that passion."

And lo and behold He did—a deep-throated, tear-spilling, grinning feeling of love that never goes away.

It made perfect sense that Nancy would be my friend now. For God was doing a work in me. He was opening me up, freeing me to face needed change without being afraid. He was encouraging me, reassuring me, giving me all sorts of reasons why I could take the plunge and trust Him to change those initial negative thoughts into positive ones.

All along, watching this from a short distance, was Ron, my

sweet, patient, and also optimistic husband. For thirty-six years—*thirty-six years*—he has patiently modeled optimism to me, made me laugh when I complained, and regularly counseled me out of feeling overwhelmed. He and Nancy made a great team without even realizing it.

Maybe it all just came together. Maybe I couldn't even begin to let go of my fears until my passion for God brought me to the place where abandonment to His plan sounded better than the alternative . . . and these two people showed me how to work that out in real life. With Ron on one side, Nancy on the other, and God in charge, I couldn't stay the same.

Now *this* is my game plan, something I'm really trying to make into a habit: when I'm tempted to obsess over a future responsibility, or when I get buried under paper piles as I am wont to do, or when something really tragic takes over my mind, I make myself concentrate on being thankful. First and foremost, that God is over it all, even down to the piles, and that my prayers will affect the situation. It is quite amazing how thanksgiving can radically change my perspective in a matter of minutes. I'm not great at it yet, but I'm amazed at the distance I've traveled.

Oh my. It just hit me. Maybe my first thoughts *are* becoming positive ones!

clutch them to my heart

I've finally figured out who I am in Christ: ordinary like the worm and extraordinary like the Son. Saint and sinner. A package of faults and fears balanced out by grand and gracious personhood, a true daughter of God.

I refuse to get too worked up about these apparent contradictions of personality. Aren't we all a conglomeration of nature and nurture, smart and stupid? Yet we have blind spots and annoying idiosyncrasies, some of which really need to be dealt with if we're going to be all that we can be, and certainly all that God wants us to be.

The most significant lessons we learn in life, I've concluded, are not the ones we learn once and that's that. Rather, they're the ones that keep coming up, the ones that address our blind spots, the ones that are so weighty they break our hearts when they take so long to learn. Such is another lesson Nancy kept grilling into me: *get your eyes off yourself!*

I know I should! But you wouldn't know it to listen to me. Am I the only one who sees everything in the whole entire world in terms of how it affects herself? Am I the only one who has a me-centered dialogue running through her head every day, everywhere? Is that a Mary idiosyncrasy or a woman-thing? Or is it simply the annoying universal sin of self-preoccupation?

I fear it's the latter. Saint Augustine wrote, "O Lord, deliver me from this lust of always vindicating myself." And, I would add, of always *considering* myself.

"Getting your eyes off yourself" is a logical next step after an attitude adjustment. The positive-attitude stuff gets you feeling comfortable enough about the world at large that you can tackle something as enormous as ego.

> *I've finally figured out who I am in Christ: ordinary like the worm and extraordinary like the Son.*

Nancy was baffled to hear me speak disparagingly, and so often, about myself. Baffled but also irritated, and not just about my self-esteem issues. More about the fact that anyone with such a self-focus leaves the rest of the world behind.

In advertising school I learned that one of the primary require-ments of selling is to take notice when you walk in a person's office or home. Take notice of the details, because that will give you a good idea of what interests them, what to talk to them about. All my life I've been interested in what makes people tick.

I remember driving into Shanghai at midnight on a bus

and seeing how different their lives were than mine, and having such a feeling of wanting to clutch them to my heart and take them all home. I had so much and they had so little.

So it started out as a casual thing, and it turned into something I do deliberately. I try to pick the brains of people; I try to find out what makes them tick. For a brief second when I meet someone, I try to imagine their lives. Does someone reach over and hug them? Are they awakening to a cold empty existence and their day never changes from that? What can I do or say from the Lord for that one second that will make them want to wake up tomorrow?

It used to be deliberate, and now it's automatic. Does this person need someone to come into their life today to be an encourager?

Nancy had the personality and experience—and the chutzpah—to jump right into our lives and relationships, invited or not. She was interested in everything about nearly everybody and had that brilliant ability to turn every conversation back to you. She picked up on signals given freely as well as those submerged in a quiet personality and drew conclusions from those signals. Then she looked for ways to open up conversations, and from there she built relationships.

Her conversation starters were the typical ones: *Tell me about your kids. What got you into landscape maintenance? How did you happen to end up in San Diego? Where'd you get those jazzy sneakers?* She probably stayed with this line of conversation with the people she didn't see very often, but with those she knew well, she asked question after question and actually remembered the answers.

It seems the beginning point of getting my eyes off myself is observation and investigation, asking questions and doing my best to remember the person's answers, starting with everyone's name. Certainly, entering a conversation more intent on finding out about others rather than waiting for them to ask about me makes sense.

Or maybe the beginning point is finding that "feeling of wanting to clutch them to my heart and take them all home."

George Eliot once wrote, "What do we live for, if not to make the world less difficult for each other." Now that's a motivation. The lessening of a burden, the lifting of cares and concerns. Is it even possible to "make the world less difficult" for another if our first consideration is ourselves?

This is my new prayer: *Lord, now that You've given me a passion for You, give me a passion for others, a feeling to go with Your command to "love one another." Help me be obedient, and flood me at the same time with that remarkable love of Yours that sees everyone as precious, valuable, and worth my while.*

hand in hand

For the longest time Nancy was known as "the little old lady who lives on the boat." Then Lynn was diagnosed with bone-marrow cancer. That was just about the time Nancy appeared on my radar screen.

All of a sudden these adventurous sailors with a considerable sea story in their past were tied to that pier in more ways than one. Nancy's friends, knowing the stuff within her, watched for that positive attitude, hoping the burden of caring for Lynn wouldn't drain the light from her eyes.

Nearly all their married life Lynn and Nancy had lived on the water and traveled when it suited them—and now Lynn found it difficult simply to climb the cabin stairs. Their freedom to leave and explore and stretch themselves at a moment's notice was gone.

But Nancy was learning to keep her eyes open to any way God might lift her spirits. The day of Lynn's first chemotherapy appointment left her pretty overwhelmed—with his condition, of course, but also with the prospect of having to take over the responsibility of the boat . . . the varnishing, the engine maintenance, all the wiring and hoses that connected everything together. She really didn't see how she could manage it all by herself.

hand in hand

That night she finished a roll of paper towels and fished in the darkness of their floating cabin for a new roll. She always bought plain white paper goods to go with their red, white, and blue decor—no colors, no pictures, no cute little sayings—and as she pulled the first roll out of a two-roll package she found she'd bought the wrong ones. Not only did *pink flowers* catch her eye but *cute little sayings* as well. It was the last straw—a silly one, but a sure sign of the stress she'd been under. She flung the roll across the room in a fit of frustration and sat down to cry.

She wrote, "The Lord allowed me to have my pity party until my faucet of tears dribbled down to a slow leak. Then I felt as though He reached out to me, and I imagined that He took my hand. 'Nancy,' my heart heard Him say in a quiet but firm voice. 'I love you, and I am right here. I am your best friend. You can always talk to Me, and I will listen to you and help you. You will never be alone, and when the time comes, I will guide your decisions.'"

All of a sudden these adventurous sailors with a considerable sea story in their past were tied to that pier in more ways than one.

She went to pick up the towels in a sweeter frame of mind. As she unrolled a sheet, she read line after line of words that touched her in her deepest need: "Friendship is a special gift." "Love is sharing." "No act of love however small is ever wasted." And she mentally ticked off all the friends she could call at any hour of the day or night and the myriad sweet voices on the phone offering love and prayers.

She crawled into bed beside her sleeping husband, profoundly comforted, shaking her head in wonder at the funny little ways God was making His presence real in her heartache.

The next morning she needed another roll of towels and reached for the open package.

"In the sunny light of day, I knew the pink-flowered roll was a special gift from God," she said. "Because when I looked at the other roll, nestled in the torn cellophane, it was plain white."

Of course, being a writer, she had to *do* something with this experience. So she wrote it all down in a letter to the paper-towel company, and somehow her story was picked up by PAX television for a series of episodes they were doing on miracles. A film crew came to San Diego and filmed the whole incident with Nancy and Lynn in the starring roles. I have the videotape to prove it.

It was easy to see how someone like Lynn could sweep a girl off her feet. He was confident and sure, seasoned, weathered, tall and fit, courageous, and impetuous. He danced and sailed and laughed, and I bet he could cook, or at least swallow, oysters without a grimace. But very quickly he lost weight and energy, and though Nancy often commented on his crinkly, smiling blue eyes, it wasn't long before his disease took over.

But still they romanced each other in little, careful ways. She told me about the first Valentine's Day in twenty years that she and Lynn missed the dance at the yacht club just up the ramp from their boat. Somehow Lynn had managed to smuggle a heart-shaped box of chocolates on board that Nancy saw when she awoke that morning, though it served to emphasize her sadness. Sipping her coffee in the foggy air while Lynn slept, she claimed a few moments of wistful, wishful thinking.

> *I turned on an oldie-but-goody radio station. The strains of Glenn Miller's "Serenade in Blue" surrounded me with comforting familiarity. I put my right arm around my waist and held up my left arm. Then I danced all over our main cabin. My spirits soared.*
>
> *When the song ended, I faced a plaque on our bulkhead. "Forgetting those things which are behind and reaching forward to those things which are ahead, I press toward the goal for the prize of the upward call of God in Christ Jesus" (Philippians 3:13–14 NKJV).*
>
> *A fast, jitterbugging song, "In the Mood," blared from the radio. Rocking with the rhythm, I peeked down at Lynn. Hunched on the edge of our bunk, his eager feet tapped in time to the music.*

Lynn's health eventually necessitated a move to land, which he and Nancy met with resolve—choosing to revel in the two flushing toilets in the new condo rather than whimper about their land-locked location. And Nancy went out and bought a roomful of

Southern California model-home furniture, all peach and cream, wrought iron and glass.

All that remained of their sea life were several beautiful pieces of driftwood perched here and there, the ship's clock and sextant by the door, and an 8x10 photo of them walking away from on-lookers, down the dock, hand in hand.

Was it hard taking care of her husband? With surprise in her eyes she answered hotly, "No! It's a privilege."

They were always hand in hand. And Nancy made Lynn such a focus of her life that under her tender loving care, he lived nine years longer than his doctor predicted.

But it wasn't easy. Watching him deal with significant pain broke her heart. And when his mind grew feeble, it was doubly hard. Seeing him going to bed fully clothed lost its humor after a while. So did having to tell Lynn again and again where things were, despite the little signs she'd tacked up throughout the apartment. I once wondered if she worried that Lynn would take those car keys he was so fond of pocketing and go for a ride without her knowing.

Yes, she got tired and admitted to cross moments. But she didn't allow herself the luxury of self-pity or complaining, at least not in my presence, nor did I ever hear her refer to her actions as "duty." You can't get to that level of sacrifice unless you *do* take your eyes off yourself.

Someone once asked her about it. Was it hard taking care of

her husband? With surprise in her eyes, she answered hotly, "No! *It's a privilege.*"

Her example spoke volumes.

As Lynn's cancer advanced, he began to show up in church. It seemed the weaker he got, the more determined he grew to be in that front row every Sunday morning, his snowy white head towering above her little gray one.

I rarely saw Lynn before or after their move inland, even on the days our writers' group met at their place. I regret that terribly, because he died before I knew I needed to know him well.

When he was nearing the end of his life, I met Nancy's daughter, Kathy, and granddaughter, Cristina. Of course, Nancy had talked about them and her son, Johnny, endlessly to all of us. Vicki, Jennie, and I might have been her in-town family, but they were the real deal, and you could tell it in the tone of her voice and the preparations she'd make to be ready for a visit. There was no question of the true hierarchy in any of our minds. Though it was, of course, no surprise to us, it was touching to see how they loved her and how devoted they were to Lynn.

His death in 1998 was a devastating loss to Nancy. I was out of town that week, so I only heard stories of the late-night drama. Of Cristina blowing in like a tornado to crawl gently onto Lynn's bed in a final good-bye. Of Kathy going into the other bedroom to rest and then thinking, *I didn't say good night to Lynn*, and going back to do so just in time. Of Nancy falling asleep beside him where they snored in unison. Of Kathy waking her to tell her he was gone, then oh-so-very-carefully dressing him for his journey to the morgue. Of Jennie's gentle husband, Bob, praying with Nancy, then wrapping his coat and arms around her and leading her out on the balcony while Lynn's body was taken from the apartment.

And even of the hilarious moment when Nancy opened the door for the mortician to find a Johnny Cochran lookalike in a black-on-black tuxedo with a velvet-draped gurney. I heard that Kathy stared her down so she wouldn't giggle. I think it was a gift from God to them both.

I missed being part of the comfort team, missed being available to hang around and listen if she wanted to talk. I even missed the scattering of Lynn's ashes in the ocean within a circle of boats piloted by old friends and fellow sailors.

Nancy told me of subsequent times when she'd shove Lynn's hat over her short hair so she could smell him, and drive to the foggy beach to cry. In characteristic fashion she didn't talk much about all she was going through. But when she finally could, she wrote (and published several times) an article about his recliner and the process of her grief that broke us all up.

in passing
nancy bayless

On a crisp, leaves-all-over-my-doormat morning, I washed your fingerprints off the recliner. One by one by one, they disappeared.

Gone forever.

hand in hand

Life ebbed from you in this recliner. When you left, it became my sanctuary. I'd wrap your dark green terry-cloth bathrobe around my fragile frame and rest here. Tired. So tired.

All the thoughts I'd stuffed away unraveled in this recliner.

Like the day the woman came from hospice. "Mr. Bayless, you are terminally ill with less than six months to live. Do you understand?"

You grabbed the chair lever and sat straight up. "I hear you, but the Lord's in charge of when I die." Then you shoved the lever down and stretched out again. Unconcerned.

I knew you would never give up. When the pain made you wince, I knelt beside this recliner. "Are you ready to go to heaven?" You nodded.

"Do you want to go today?"

You smiled and reached out. Your hand cradled my chin. "No. Not today."

It had become our special joke. We who had flown to the outposts of the world. Sailed mighty oceans in small boats. Climbed high mountains and driven our VW van wherever our spirits led us. We had pushed "delete" on our adventure buttons.

After the monstrous cancer wormed its way into our lives, in order to give us hope, I'd plan trips. I would ask if you wanted to go, and you always said, "Yes! Of course I want to go!"

I outlined the entire trip, then I'd say, "Do you want to go today?"

You'd smile and pat me. "No. Not today."

In this recliner I remembered the moment you took my hand and led me into your heart. You stuck my hand in the pocket of your jeans, then you put your arm around my waist and pointed out to sea. "There's a lot of world out there, and you should be ready to go in thirty minutes. If you don't take the things you need with you, learn to get along without them or buy new ones." I mentally saluted, stayed "on alert," and found bursting joy.

In this recliner I relived the pain that seared through me like amputation, when the strangers came to take you away from me. During those awful moments the protective love of my precious Christian friend enfolded me. He steered me out onto our balcony and held me from behind . . . clutching his jacket over my trembling shoulders.

Moonlight drenched a clear-eyed midnight sky, as I envisioned two dramas unfolding at the same instant. In heaven Jesus stood and held out His hand. Here on earth you let my hand go and took His.

In this recliner I thought about the first morning without you. Curled in a single bed with my daughter's arms wrapped around me. Our roles reversed.

In this recliner I made up imaginary scenes to cope with my agony. I didn't want to see anyone, and I planned what I would do if the doorbell rang. I'll run. Vault over our bal-

cony. Dash to our van and head west. When I see our ocean, I'll park, stagger across the sand, and fall on my face, sobbing. The fog will collect around me, and no one will see me there. As waves crash against the shore, the fog will creep away and the sun will peek through snowy clouds drifting across an amazing blue sky. I'll stop crying, turn on my back, and look up to where you are. Oh, it's a glorious day! This day when you stopped breathing.

The doorbell rang. I wiggled from the recliner and dropped your bathrobe on the floor. I looked longingly at the balcony. If I jump, I'll probably shatter and break my neck. So I smiled and opened the door.

In this recliner blessings from our friends and families ran rampant through my heart, along with the delicious feeling of having my son, from across the sea, beside me. His ever-capable hands readied the basket filled with your ashes so I could scatter them over our ocean.

I asked you once what you wanted me to do for you if you died first. You pulled me into your arms and said, in your inimitable way, "I don't care. I won't be there."

But your unique humor prevailed as people came from all points of the compass for your memorial service. A seal jumped twice, right in the middle of your ashes! You would have loved that. . . .

On a sweltering, overcast day, when I'd been a widow for three weeks, I left the recliner. I put on your hat and drove freeways frantic with traffic. Parked our van at a friend's house. Climbed aboard trains and huddled in buses. Hugged grandchildren and buried my face in the soft hair of great-grandchildren. Surrounded by so many giggles, it seemed ungrateful to be sad, but I still needed your recliner. Sometimes sadness stunned me . . . while joy nuzzled my toes.

I wound my way back to our van and headed west. Dense fog embraced our ocean. I pulled to the side of the road as mist swirled around me. I opened the window to let some in. I wonder if any of your ashes are nested among those rocks? I want to go over there, drop on my knees, and claw the sand away. All I need is a tiny fragment of you.

Tears dribbled over my steering wheel. The fog lifted. I held your hat against my cheek. It smelled like you. I checked in the rearview mirror and put it on at a rakish angle like you used to do. Then I drove south.

"Surrounded by so many giggles, it seemed ungrateful to be sad."

Back home, in the recliner, I rocked your bathrobe against my heart. God opened His wonderful arms, and I crawled in. I drowned in worship music blasting from my stereo and put red hearts on my calendar for each church service. My telephone bill peaked out at well over three figures. I crammed my hours with doing stuff, until one icy, frosty-windows day, I realized I didn't need your recliner in my bedroom anymore, so I moved it to my guest room. I looked at it often. Sat in it . . . reclined in it . . . stroked it . . . prayed in it . . . cried in it . . . talked to it. I wore your bathrobe around the house over my clothes.

The months raced by so fast it surprised me. On a radiant, see-to-our-ocean day, with painstaking love, I placed your bathrobe in my washing machine. After my dryer fluffed it dry, I smoothed it with my hands, over and over and over. Then I hung it in the guest-room closet.

That night I studied your recliner. Looked at it with appreciative eyes. Sat down. Stretched out. Sat up. Rubbed my hands over the soft leather where your fingers had clutched life. Finally, I reached for the telephone and dialed a familiar number. Within an hour . . . strong arms of a friend lifted your recliner out of my life.

I hugged myself and smiled. Sadness may still stun me . . . but joy floods my soul. This doesn't really surprise me. The Bible tells me that, "Weeping may endure for a night, but joy comes in the morning."

Sometimes I forget and automatically reach for your hand. You aren't there. You are gone, like your fingerprints. So I take God's hand. He is always with me, and He is my hope and my joy.

too lonely for dancing

Though Nancy remained the same optimistic, free-spirited nineteen-year-old, Lynn's death initiated a significant shift in how the four of us related. She had always been the confidante, the advice-giver, the listener. Now she began to lean on the three of us in a more deliberate way, confiding more openly in us, letting us in on some of her own aching heart and adding some levels of revelation that we were missing before.

One night she and I went to a wedding at our church. Jennie and Vicki were there with their husbands, but Ron was out of town. I was glad to have Nancy with me, because once again I wondered if I fit in. I watched her flit from table to table eagerly greeting too many friends to count. For all I knew, she was having a marvelous time. But this is how she described it later:

> At last night's wedding, watching nearly everyone dance, I found myself surprised by an overwhelming sense of loss. I could not force my feet to join the gang of swaying bodies. I didn't want to dance alone as many were doing. I didn't want to dance with another woman, and the thought of physical contact with a man made me cringe. I longed for

my husband's strong arms and to feel his firm leading as he whirled me around and around. I took a snapshot out of my wallet and went into the bathroom. The photo showed us swing dancing. Serpentine streamers hung between our bodies, but our hands clung together. My husband had on his wonderful smile. I wanted to sit on the toilet and bawl.

Instead, I counted the blessings of joyous nights lost in the rhythm of the music and each other. I put on bright red lipstick and rejoined the throng.

When I got home, I crawled into our bed, sipped hot chocolate, and remembered our wedding . . .

I rarely heard Nancy refer to her status as a widow. She seemed so ready to go, so ready to try something new, so ready to learn. I didn't often consider what she might be thinking at home, every night, alone. Then she wrote this and read it to us one day as we sat around the little table in her kitchen:

I despise the word widow. *It is so descriptive. Everyone knows what it means, even kids. The first time I had to put the word on a form, I felt like someone on the dole. Someone society thought of as a drag. I do feel blessed that the Bible says God takes care of widows, but that's about the only plus to the title.*

A widow is someone who lives alone . . . gets invited to functions by caring friends . . . but sits in the backseat looking at the backs of the couples' heads, wanting to bawl or jump out of the car and hitchhike home. A widow always makes it necessary to add an extra place at the table, so that the people who should be sitting next to one another are not, and the widow is between the honeymooners or the guests of honor.

I refuse to eat in restaurants alone, and mostly eat standing up at my kitchen counter, or take my food to my bed and watch TV while I wolf it down. And I have yet to go to the movies with a single, senior, price-is-right ticket.

Having said all that, I have learned to come home to an empty house with eager footsteps, enjoy my solitude, and count as a precious blessing the friendships of women like you three who reach out continually to include me in their lives.

When we heard Nancy's words, we sat stunned, grieved, our mouths round in surprise. Vicki said, with all the pathos possible in only three words, "*I'm so sorry.*" We all felt like that, and could hardly believe we'd missed something so significant in our dear friend's life, something we should have anticipated. And, as we talked about it in front of her, we confessed we didn't know what to do about it.

Nancy quickly cut in. "There's nothing you can do about it, and you shouldn't feel guilty. You are always there for me. Always! Widowhood is a process I must go through. It is an amputation. Like losing my right hand. It heals, but I always look down and know it's gone."

too lonely for dancing

If Ron dies before I do . . . well, I can hardly bear to think about it.

He asked me to marry him two weeks after our first date (though we'd known each other well for a year). I was not ready to commit so quickly—I still had a few other crushes to deal with—but he wore me down, and we married a year later. No one ever sat me down to explain the significance of marriage, the work it would take, the inherent heartaches and joys and self-sacrifice that come with a lifetime commitment. I didn't know anything, and

> "Widowhood is an amputation. It heals, but I always look down and know it's gone."

neither did he. Somehow we muddled through our very difficult first year. (There is a benefit to having a rough beginning—there's no way to go but up.) And we continue to muddle through communications and expectations like most couples.

In my opinion, he's the secret of our lasting marriage. His positive thinking pulls me up; his kindness gives me room to be my melancholy self—yet encourages a positive attitude. He is the steady rock whose response to life is never a surprise.

And I wonder how I could manage without him. (I recently heard about a couple married for seventy years who died within three hours of each other—I'm praying for *that*.) When Ron travels I get a taste of it, I suppose. But widowhood, when the short separations are replaced with interminable ones, when there isn't any snoring to drown out, scares me.

Once Nancy and I discussed this, and of course, we came at

it from two different points of view. She told me she had prayed that Lynn would die first because she couldn't stand the thought of him having to be alone. It crushed me that that thought hadn't even entered my mind regarding my own husband.

Ron will be fine if I die first, grieving but fine. I doubt he's given it a moment's thought. But I'm the analyzer, the worrier. I've already imagined what it might be like. If he dies first, will I get up in the morning when there's no one there to see it? If my soul mate is not under my roof and in my bed anymore, won't I be too lonely for dancing, just like Nancy?

She isn't here to read these words. She wouldn't want me to write so glumly about an unknown future, as if I'm setting myself up for just those reactions. She wouldn't want me to make assumptions about life as if God were an outside figure, sitting in His easy chair, passive and uninvolved.

One day at lunch with the three of us, Nancy, always on a quest to protect the marriages around her, climbed up on that soapbox without leaving her chair. With Lynn gone and extra time on her hands, she seemed almost obsessive about making sure our marriages were in tiptop shape. So over salad and hot bread, she told us, one by one, how she thought we were relating to our husbands.

She was not very flattering to me and to my marriage, and she made me squirm. She wanted to see Ron and me holding hands more, sitting closer, physically connecting whenever she saw us, and she implied our public persona mirrored our private one. I bristled at the idea that she thought she knew how Ron and I connected to each other at home. I told her so. She held her ground. She was convinced that any relationship, solid or problematic, could be enhanced or healed—and measured—by touching.

Over salad and hot bread, she told us, one by one, how she thought we were relating to our husbands.

You bet it was hard to sit under her watchful eye, to be forced to examine my marriage when I didn't think it needed such close examination. But she did make me think.

Though I was slow to the point of inertia to make the connection, I finally remembered one particular incident that applied. One night Ron and I were lounging in front of the TV. Our good old dog, Homer, crawled up on the couch between my legs and lay across my chest. Absent-mindedly, I did what anyone in a similar situation would do—I scratched his ears and rubbed his belly. And then I heard this prolonged sigh coming from deep in Ron's chair.

"What's that about?" I asked him.

"I wish you'd do that to me."

Touching became a favorite subject for Nancy. She actually worked up an entire seminar on the subject, including research on monkeys and babies and how important physical contact is to the development of a healthy psyche, human or not. It became one of her signature recommendations for marital staleness or difficulty.

> *When I first met Lynn, he said he wasn't affectionate, but over the years that followed, through constant touching on my part, he became one of the world's most affectionate men. We always held hands when we walked, and I rarely passed him in the house or anywhere when he didn't reach out and touch me.*
>
> *Touching is an unequivocal form of love. We used to go to the mall and people watch. We often saw wives way ahead of their husbands, berating them over their shoulders. The men usually looked resigned, embarrassed, or bored. I wanted to call out, "Zip your lips, woman! Walk next to him! Hold hands! Touching works miracles!"*

I took what she said to heart, albeit with a touch of rebelliousness. Funny, just having that word on my brain began to make a difference. So much so that just a month ago I heard Molly tell someone that she loves how her dad and mom "touch each other all the time."

Not bad, huh?

On one of our sojourns Nancy and I talked about the need for couples to make alone time a priority. I'd said to her before, when she'd refused my invitation to dinner so Ron and I could be alone, "Trust me to protect my own marriage." But she seemed a little leery of my judgment.

That conversation led to a discussion on the pros and cons of answering machines. She didn't like them very much (particularly the message we had at the time that said simply, "You've reached the Jensons. We're screening our calls.") because of the way technology further distances people, which she connected to the breakdown of communication in marriage.

"Wait a minute," I challenged her. "Answering machines *give* us alone time! It's the only way we can get through dinner without interruption!" She reluctantly agreed, then read me a paragraph she'd brought along about Lynn, giving me another picture of his charm.

Our alone times were the sweetest blessings of our marriage. Oddly enough, I don't ever remember hearing Lynn suggest we go out to lunch or take in a movie or walk in the woods. Rather, he'd amble into the room and crook his finger at me and wiggle it. Even though he often picked inopportune times to do this, my heart pumped with excitement when he'd take my hand and open the car door. One time we found ourselves screaming with joy from the top of a Ferris wheel. Another time we stood awestruck at the end of a long breakwater while salt spray drenched us. One early morning he woke me by outlining my face with his forefinger. As I opened my eyes,

what an old friend taught me about life

he smiled and crooked his finger. That morning we watched
circus animals unload from boxcar after boxcar.

Nancy had been grieving Lynn's death long before it actually happened and, though I don't think she was surprised by the depth of her feelings, I do think she discovered some things about widowhood she didn't anticipate.

For one, she hated going home to an empty house. Though she didn't mind being alone once inside, opening that door to no one really got to her. Maybe because of that reluctance, maybe because she'd been house-and-husband-bound for so long, when the time came, off she went, by herself—on a train to Colorado and the Continental Divide, to Florida and Idaho to visit all the grandchildren and great-grandchildren, to Northern California to visit old friends. She wrote tales of her

> *She met the challenges of traveling alone at seventy-five without admitting to any fear or self-consciousness.*

"trips with Jesus," met people of all ages, in all stages, all races and most creeds, and befriended them all, collecting names and faces and stories to share with us once she returned. She met the challenges of traveling alone at seventy-five without admitting to any fear or self-consciousness, and once more we were enthralled by her life and in awe of her strength.

When she settled back into a routine in San Diego, God dropped Stephanie into her life. Twenty-something Stephanie lived forty-five minutes away but worked at our church, which was just around the corner from Nancy's house. So occasionally, when her schedule got tight, she'd stay overnight. Eventually she moved in and became Nancy's roommate for a year. Stephanie filled that physical-presence void that Lynn left, and Nancy loved her deeply.

Though they were nearly fifty years apart in age, Nancy's ability to bend her heart and lifestyle toward another meant that she and Stephanie lived like college girls, talking and laughing late into the night, making ice-cream runs to Ben & Jerry's, and dancing around the condo (with Stephanie's teddy bear as the male lead) to the great Big Band tunes. Nancy had the pleasure of watching Stephanie fall in love with a young man in *two weeks* (hmm, Nancy's influence?), joyfully helping to orchestrate the prewedding plans and sitting with the family on the big day.

But when Stephanie married, Nancy found herself alone again.

call me and let's go play

Nancy collected people, and it started long before her widowhood. Her heart reached out to every lonely soul and to bunches of others who caught her eye. Though she had her share of books and was admittedly fond of shoes, she had no other collections. Her counters were clear, and I can attest to the fact that her closets held no secret stashes of trinkets. People were her obsession—men, women, children; all ages, races, and dress codes.

So when she admonished me to "get my eyes off myself," I took a little closer look at how she did it. First, I observed that she was as interested in talking with the guy trimming the bushes outside her front door as with the rich and famous (and she had stories to tell about the famous). I don't know if she actually planned out how she was going to forge a new friendship, or if it just came so naturally and unselfconsciously that it was inevitable. Yes, she had trained herself to observe and remember; but, really, I think she just did it. She began. She made the first move. She didn't wait until it was convenient or until she had good hair.

"I don't feel that I so literally love people," she told me. "That's not it. But I feel a need to reach out to people."

call me and let's go play

"That's an interesting distinction," I said, "because I know you don't love everybody you talk to."

"God has given me the ability to treat them as if I loved them. And so not only do I not know whom I love, but they don't either. Again, it's not important. It's about them. I could point out to you people from my day—the guy at the counter at the post office. He just loves to see me for a minute. It makes his day. And then you go down the street and you find somebody else. You can always find somebody. I think my heart is always seeking to reach out and touch someone with something. Just something that will be in their minds as they go through their day."

> She waited until she'd heard all about you before she talked about herself.

Potential was much more appealing to her than titles and reputation, though she was known to drop a name or two. People's stories fascinated her. She wanted to know how you got the way you were. And then she wanted to challenge you to be the best you could be.

She looked you in the eye and asked endless questions, often pointed ones that made you face an issue you might be avoiding. And she waited until she'd heard all about you before she talked about herself. All this disarmed people who might normally be guarded—even the famous.

"Did I ever tell you about the time Steve McQueen kissed

me?" she asked one morning. I was navigating heavy traffic on the 5 through Los Angeles, and I nearly drove into the retaining wall.

"What?" I asked incredulously. I wanted to look at her and see if she was baiting me but couldn't take my eyes off the road.

"Did I ever tell you about Steve McQueen?"

My partner, Joe, and I returned to La Paz, Mexico, from delivering a boat to San Diego. We had left Joe's boat, an old Block Island ketch, anchored in La Paz Harbor under the watchful eye of a fellow cruiser. Darkness clung to the sandy beach when we arrived and whistled to our friend. He turned on a light aboard his boat and climbed into his dinghy. Another man climbed in with him. When they reached us, our friend said, "This is Steve. He finished the Baja 500 race today and he's hungry. Why don't you leave your stuff in my dinghy, and we'll go to town and get a hamburger."

When we reached the lighted restaurant, Steve's blue eyes smiled at us as he signed an autograph for the waitress. While we munched our burgers, he asked us all kinds of questions about our ketch. "Will you take me for a sail tomorrow?" (You bet we will!)

The next morning I rowed to town and went to his hotel. He stood by the desk talking on the phone. When he saw me, he put the receiver down and said, "I can't go. They want me back in L.A. I'm so sorry."

I touched his arm. "Take care of yourself," I whispered, then went out on the sidewalk and wanted to have a temper

tantrum. I had walked about a block when I heard him call-
ing my name. He ran up behind me, put his hands on my
shoulders, and kissed my cheek.

"I hope I'll find you guys somewhere in the world so you
can take me sailing. OK?"

My body wanted to melt into the sidewalk. "OK," I
murmured. Then he turned and ran back . . . out of my life.

What intrigued me most about Nancy's people collection were the children. Try as I might, I can't get kids to warm up to me like she could. Or like Ron can, for that matter.

Once at a high-school basketball game, Ron and I were standing up against the wall watching the action. Along came a mom and a boy about five to stand next to us. Ron started an animated conversation with this boy, asking him if he went to school at this particular high school, if he worked there, or if he was married. That tickled the child, of course, and provided some great diversion from a not-so-great game.

The next day I was in my chiropractor's waiting room and in walked another mom and a little girl. I thought I'd try Ron's tactic, and I asked the child if she worked for the chiropractor. She stared at me, incredulous, and turned around to bury her head in her mother's skirt.

But Nancy was a charmer. "Most of the children at church have let me into their hearts," Nancy wrote. "Little girls pirouette across the doormat so that I can see how far out their dresses twirl. Boys look me in the eye and grin when I admire their ties or jazzy shoes. I get to wiggle loose teeth and to see the holes after the teeth have come out. Children show me their Bibles and ask if I know the stories they are learning in Sunday school. Many of the teenagers seem genuinely glad to see me on their way into church."

Nancy had such a beeline to kids' hearts that I couldn't have been happier when my own children took up with her.

Matt loved the fact that he could be himself with Nancy. He describes her as a "principled person who left room for irreverence," and it was the freedom he felt with her, to joke or speak seriously, that he loved the most. That's not to say she refused to pry into his personal life. Far from it. But he knew she "had some grandmother in her," so he took what she said and respected it, though with the proverbial grain of salt.

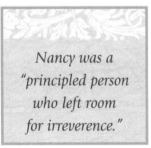

Nancy was a "principled person who left room for irreverence."

Nancy talked Matt into teaching her how to play the piano, thinking that in no time she'd be amusing us all with golden oldies. It proved to be a little more complicated than she thought, though, so they happily switched to dancing. I'd see them at church, off to the side, getting in a few steps. Matt treated her as a peer—like she treated him—and they teased, poked, and tickled each other. He'd stop in at her place to say hi, and she'd keep tabs on his dating relationships. She called him "Matéo" and he called her "Darlin'."

Molly fit right in with Nancy's *joie de vivre*, and they became immediate friends. And at just the right time. Molly was in a serious relationship with a young man, and I needed someone to meet him and give me her impression. She became a sounding board throughout their engagement—and their breakup. Nancy, who always loved a good wedding, was really disappointed. In fact, she seemed so impetuous about relationships I could imagine her thinking, *Why ruin a good love story, you silly kids!*

Friendships between kids/teenagers and seniors are pretty uncommon these days. You might see it in a family, but rarely do you see what we saw with Nancy and her young entourage. So many kids are afraid of older people; I think seniors can do a lot to dispel that fear. Nancy certainly did, and I bet the kids she loved will grow up with a much healthier view of aging. And the aged.

"Call me and let's go play," she'd say. And she'd take you to lunch or to tea at a fancy hotel, giving the young girls the opportunity to dress up and try out their manners.

We'd hit plays and movies and follow Molly's band around town. I heard rumors from Vicki and Jennie of mud baths and spa treatments, and of nights playing cards and board games with their families. However serious the competition became, Nancy had a way of making it fun, of celebrating the childlike behavior of the kids and drawing childlike behavior out of self-conscious adults. Who needed to "discover your inner child" with her around to do it for you? She even applauded the night Jennie drove a group of teenage girls on a TPing mission and pushed her for all the details the next day.

Our kids could talk to Nancy about anything. (What a gift it is for our kids to have other adults in whom they can confide!) If what they said elicited a rebuke, which it might, they could take it from her easier than from us. Perhaps because they'd heard her stories. Perhaps because she had a way of listening and nodding with amusement and recognition that relieved a little of the pressure.

Did they glamorize Nancy's past just a little? Probably. It sounded so romantic and adventurous to think of a woman striking out on her own, living in exotic places, sailing away with the man of her dreams, and living happily ever after like the fairy tales. I knew our children eagerly lapped up her stories and didn't always consider Nancy's testimony or take the time to put it all into perspective—that her world travels were kicked off by a failed marriage, that her ties to family were looser than any of us would be comfortable with, that it took a few tries to find her heart's desire and settle down with the right man.

Defending our more conventional lifestyles sounded stuffy. And safe. But I think the lessons our kids drew from her had more to do with the attitudes she lived by than with the earlier choices she had made. They saw courage in her, and perseverance. They saw acceptance and overwhelming patience with people and all their foibles. They saw a well-developed understanding of human nature and what it takes to live victoriously with so much that could be considered insurmountable in your past.

They saw a life that Christ rescued and a woman who loved Him for it.

the weight of tragedy

"Can't I talk you into a Dove Bar this time?" Nancy asked one day as we pulled up to a one-pump gas station/minimart in a small town. It was the fall of 2001, a few years after Lynn's death. We were old traveling buddies by this time, with clearly defined roles and well-established habits. Even to the ice cream. But that didn't mean there was no room for a little persuasion.

"Come on," she said. "Have one just this once."

"Nope. No Dove Bars for me. I'd rather get a good old ice-cream sandwich like I always do."

"But Mary, Dove Bars are so rich and wonderful."

"Nancy," I said, "I'm not quite enough woman for a Dove Bar."

She laughed for quite a while at that, but it only served to reinforce her commitment to get me to change my thinking about myself. She wanted to see me take risks, do new things, even break a rule or two. Like eating dessert first.

With Lynn gone, Jennie, Vicki, and I got her undivided attention. We were her day job. She had work to do in our lives.

She and I were on our way to Santa Barbara the last weekend of September 2001. I'd agreed months before, with all the angst that accompanies such agreements, to speak for a pastor's wife we both loved at her church-women's brunch.

It had been a horrifying few weeks, with 9/11 and the creeping fear that was overtaking America. The day the towers were hit, just after 6:00 a.m., California time, I was having my morning coffee and quiet time. The phone rang. It was Nancy. "Turn on your television," she said quickly. I was not happy to have been interrupted and had no desire to turn on my TV.

"Why?" I whined.

"Turn on your TV," she demanded, then hung up with no further explanation. And I turned on my TV.

Like everyone else in America, none of us really knew how to talk about it. We all checked in with our extended families and friends. TV sets blared from our homes, and we read and listened to everything we could find—and cried and cried and cried.

But life went on, though people continued to be rather skittish about travel and collecting in any one spot. I wondered if anyone would show up at this brunch I had been fretting about for so long. My topic was "stillness," a significant enough subject without 9/11. Now the weight of tragedy was heavy upon me. How could I convince the women that stillness was possible when I was having all this trouble finding it myself?

All the way up—three hours worth—I talked this through with Nancy, not just what I needed to say but how inadequate I was feeling. Finally, she blurted out, "Get your eyes off yourself!"

The vehemence of her outburst startled me. It's a good thing I had both hands on the wheel.

"Mary! You're coming at this from the wrong direction," she said. "What you're doing up in Santa Barbara is not about how well you say what you say. It's about those women! What do *they* need? What does God want to say to them? Can't you get yourself out of the way?"

Not yet, it seemed. I had one more thing I wanted to discuss, so I took a deep breath and brought up an area I've struggled with since childhood—a slight stutter. Maybe I was trying to justify my unease, maybe I got a little defensive. Who knows. But this was the first time I had really, fully opened up about it with *anyone* outside my family. It's funny how guarded we can be about certain things in our lives, things that we don't need to be guarded about. It was a significant enough moment to me that I can remember the hills we were driving through, the way the sun glanced off our windshield, and the length of the shadows in the late afternoon.

Nancy had heard me speak in front of people before, and the revelation surprised her. It's rarely a problem, but I know it's there, and when I'm vulnerable, it rattles around in my conscious and subconscious mind like an annoying, yippy little dog that you can't silence permanently because it belongs to your favorite aunt.

It surfaced when I was in grade school. It didn't ruin my life, but it did make every class where grades depended upon recitation and reading (like French) rather gut wrenching. I've spent a lifetime compensating for it. I convinced my high-school French teacher to bypass me during the recitation section of class and let me meet with her afterward for a private session. Can you imagine what my classmates thought, when one after the other, right down the rows, they recited their answers, and Mademoiselle Dykes skipped over *me* with no explanation? What a prima donna.

No doubt repressed memories of French class figured into my speaking insecurities. Nancy had never been aware of it, and though she didn't discount my experience, she didn't understand the weight of it on me and the history of its wily influence in my life. Her solution to what was not an easy revelation was the positive thinking mantra of Norman Vincent Peale. "Tell yourself," she said to me, "'I speak with fluidity.'"

As those of you with similar struggles know, there's more to it than that.

Moses is my best friend—a stutterer with an insecurity complex. He's the one I want to meet first in heaven. God was so patient with him, bringing along Aaron for support, letting Moses use whatever props he needed . . . until he began to rise to the occasion and live up to God's opinion of him. Reading Exodus and watching Moses move from frightened mouthpiece to powerful leader is one of my favorite sections of the Bible.

I have no such leadership aspirations, but I, like all of us, have occasions to rise to, and each time God and I talk it over, I get what Moses got. Patience, gentle guidance, understanding, hope.

what an old friend taught me about life

The women's brunch was in the church's main meeting room in an old packing house that had been artfully transformed into a rather funky and inviting, if enormous, space. Even with 9/11 on our minds, the women were shining with intensity, purpose, and anticipation. Friendly smiles greeted Nancy and me, and one woman even told me I had beautiful skin, though the context of our conversation implied "for my age." Still, it lifted my spirits.

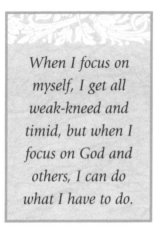

When I focus on myself, I get all weak-kneed and timid, but when I focus on God and others, I can do what I have to do.

The day before, a friend had relayed to me a vision of Jesus standing tall above the towers, encouraging the ones who escaped to hurry along and spreading His love and tenderness over those who didn't. Someday we'll know why and what God was doing; for the moment it was a beautiful picture of His sovereignty and compassion. I could hardly wait to share it.

Nancy's reprimand did what she intended it to do. It reminded me again that when I focus on myself, I get all weak-kneed and timid, but when I focus on God and others, I can do what I have to do. Gone were the nerves; what could I do now anyway but deliver what God had already put on my heart and in my notes? And really, all I had to do was look in their sweet faces and open my mouth. As with Moses, once I put myself aside, it was all up to Him.

the weight of tragedy

It's taken me a long time to admit it, but I talk too much, stutter or no. They say men use ten thousand words a day and women twenty-five thousand, which you'd think would give me a little leeway. It might be a stereotype that women talk more than men; yet stereotypes are built out of observation, so there you have it.

It has been a growing revelation to me, but I'm beginning to see that I have a habit of processing out loud—giving a little color commentary to the day, reminding my loved ones to wear sweaters, reciting directions, worrying, filling in the silence. You'd think that wouldn't be so annoying.

I wonder if it was this constant processing that prompted Nancy's impression of me. Was I unknowingly spilling out everything I was thinking at the time? If I'd realized what I was doing, and had kept my mouth shut a little more often, would she have come to the same conclusions?

Probably, because, as she was so fond of quoting: "As a man thinks in his heart, so is he." That's the convicting part. I might have been able to hide anxiety and self-preoccupation if I kept quiet (*Even a fool seems wise if he keeps his mouth shut*), but the underlying issues, and how I continued to let them affect me, remained.

talk of disquieting things

Elated but reflective, Nancy and I headed home from Santa Barbara the next morning. I couldn't shake the feeling that we had been part of something significant with all those women. September 11 changed us all. It was my generation's Pearl Harbor as Nancy said, and maybe God used our presence there to do a little healing. Yet there was no denying the little cloud that hovered over our heads. It went with us on the road.

Our earlier pact to take the scenic route nearly led us into trouble that evening. We had avoided Interstate 5 and taken Highway 101 to the 1, the beach road. It began for us by hugging the coastline just above Malibu, running south past the Santa Monica Pier, next to white beaches littered with the remnants of summer and just a few people on that last weekend of September. The sea flashed with the low sun, and waves chopped up as evening came. Though the traffic gridlocked around us, the slow pace meant we could enjoy the panorama of sand and surf.

But if you don't make the move inland to the interstate soon enough, you end up driving through the rougher beach towns, far enough from the ocean that you can't hear it anymore, away from the resorts and manicured lawns, on busy commercial streets that run in front of tattoo parlors and thrift shops.

We had plenty of gas and the recent memory of ice-cream bars on our lips, so we didn't have to stop until dark when we needed directions. Though we knew where we were, we weren't quite sure how to get where we wanted to go. With help we found a connecting freeway. Nancy said to go north to get us on the right track, but I, the one with the steering wheel, disagreed and turned south. That took us, two un-accompanied women in a gray Jeep with a Bible verse on the license plate, down the ramp onto Terminal Island—a spit of land southwest of Los Angeles, condemned from time to time and rumored to be sinking, that is home to oil derricks and a jail. The lights around the derricks masked the utilitarian function of the land. Maybe that's what distracted me. I guess I sat at the stoplight a little too long; maybe I waited for the green instead of "turning right on red." But the guy behind us, in a souped-up sedan, laid on his horn and roared past us with his finger in the air and a glare in his eye. Not a big deal but an uncommon occurrence for us. We didn't normally elicit such attention.

> *Nancy said to go north, but I, the one with the steering wheel, disagreed and turned south.*

Nancy suggested we blow him a *kiss*. I knew he'd follow us if we did. She thought he'd just think how much nicer it is to blow

97

a kiss than give the finger. I thought that would be the last thing on his mind.

Sometimes I wanted her to acknowledge the caution with which we have to live life these days. I didn't want to dampen her enthusiasm, but now and then I wanted her to smarten up. She told me she had plenty of street smarts—more than I do, and I agreed—and I knew she thought her plan would have worked. She said so, in no uncertain terms.

Yet as the evening and the drive went on, I found our conversation growing as troubled as our route. We talked of disquieting things. More of 9/11, anthrax scares, the wobbly stock market and all she had invested there, friends' shaky marriages. It seemed as if we'd never before had such weighty matters swirling around us, and it added a solemnity to our trip.

For a while I waited for Nancy's optimistic outlook to change the tone of our conversation. It scared me a little. I didn't really want to see her worried or frightened or nonplussed by life. I didn't want her to be like *me*, for heaven's sake. If there's one thing I loved about her, it was that I could depend on her to respond in a predictably positive way.

I needed to know that she could keep it up, regardless of the circumstances.

some kind of peace

In October of 2001 something happened to our car trips. No more forays into the mountains and overnight stops at quaint inns. No more spontaneous getaways, beach highways, and ice-cream bars on the road. Now our trips involved offices and men in white coats, and a whole different set of expectations crowded in.

One Monday morning I packed up for the day with computer, legal pad, novel, and just a few butterflies, and drove to pick Nancy up. She had a dental appointment. Though she was very self-sufficient, she wanted a chauffer because she was having two teeth pulled. I expected to be with her the whole day, comforting her, feeding her clear soup, and watching her vitals. I had visions of each of my children, loopy and strange after general anesthesia for wisdom-teeth extraction. The thought of Nancy loopy and strange, and toothless to boot, was more than a little scary.

We stopped first at her dentist where she had some out-of-mouth remodeling done on her bridges. Then we moved on to the oral surgeon's office and sat in a spacious exam room with October light pouring in the window and glimmering off the few teeth remaining in Nancy's smile.

As it turned out, Nancy's extractions were done with local

anesthesia within an hour. She introduced me to her surgeon: "Mary's my Yellow Cab."

Until this episode with her teeth, I'd heard very few comments from Nancy about her looks, her health, or her age. She was not one of those older women who traps you with details about her physical condition, and I didn't think she had a vain bone in her body. And age? It just wasn't an important enough topic to address.

But after the latest tooth extraction, she confessed to checking out her smile in the mirror more and more. And she made Vicki, Jennie, and me promise to find her dentures and shove 'em in ASAP if she died without them.

I must admit that, until recently, my thoughts on aging centered more on the outside than the inside—more on the crow's feet and saggy jowls, the floppy arms and age spots, than on any kind of weakening or lessening of bones, ligaments, muscles, or eyes, ears, and mind. How shallow.

But I'm feeling it, that weakening. And as I watched Nancy deal with her body, I upped my calcium, checked my hormones, and stepped up my flossing. Whatever it takes.

Yet, we age, grow unsteady, less agile. The same month of Nancy's dental work, I took a header smack in the middle of a busy downtown street. My family and I had just come from dinner, and on stepping into the street, I tripped on a lip of thick asphalt. I fell spread-eagled, flat out, the right side of my face slamming into the ground with some force and the rest of me following suit. It's a good thing the light was red! Stunned, I staggered on the arms of my children and husband back to the curb, where I sat in a heap trying not to pass out. (The most disconcerting part was the crazy, homeless woman shouting expletives at me for some reason, and my irate, protective son ready to take her on.)

I can't remember the last time I fell or skinned my knees or came away with a scraped chin. What an undignified way to finish off dinner! I had *scabs*!

That's what aging does to us. Slows us down, trips us up, knocks us sideways. We hope to sail through it. We envision ourselves, sleek and silver-haired, holding our own in the middle of the pack at the Boston Marathon. We say we'll refuse to give in—Jennie and Vicki keep throwing away their unsolic-

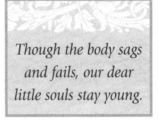

Though the body sags and fails, our dear little souls stay young.

ited, but deserved, AARP cards—but age sneaks up on us in ways we don't expect. All of a sudden we scare ourselves in the mirror, wrench our backs with the groceries, stumble in the street. I don't like it one bit.

Yet though the body sags and fails, our dear little souls stay young. The night before my wedding I told my mom I still felt like a girl. I've never forgotten her response: "Me too, honey."

Nancy dealt with age in one primary fashion: She didn't talk about it. She didn't buy senior-citizen movie tickets; she didn't appreciate "over the hill" parties with their gag gifts; she didn't allow her friends to pamper her by catering to her shuffling feet and crooked back.

She lived as if the best years were yet to come, as if middle age went on forever. Maybe with the right attitude, it does.

Regardless of my age, I want to be a girl at heart like she was, delighted with life, holding out my hands to handsome young men and dancing in the corner of the church.

One day Nancy called Vicki and left an abrupt, cryptic, gleeful message on her answering machine: "I'm on a gurney riding down the hall! Bye!"

Nancy using her cell phone on a gurney? This woman, who only dealt with homeopathic doctors, in a hospital? Who hadn't had a complete physical since her daughter, now in her fifties, was *born*? It sounded a bit alarming, but we didn't want to jump to conclusions, and we were all delighted she was willing to be examined. For some time she'd been troubled both by a persistent flu and shooting pains in her foot, and we knew the time had come for some medical intervention.

The doctor put her on antibiotics and sent her home. A few days later Nancy came clean with the rest of the story, and her foot problems paled into near insignificance. She invited the three of us over for dinner (Vicki picked up take-out Japanese), and after we ate and gossiped and laughed, she told us that her hospital visit had included an exam on a very large lump in her breast that she had ignored for a long time and that she was not going to do anything about it.

This is turning out to be a little too much like Tuesdays with Morrie, I actually thought to myself that night in her living room.

Now, you have to hear Nancy's version of the story to understand why, after a few questions, we didn't argue with her about this.

People are astonished when I tell them I haven't been to the doctor for fifty years. Doctors seem to be personally offended. Of course, it is a bit of an exaggeration. I have been to a doctor for a couple of things, but I haven't had any of the expected tests deemed absolutely necessary for women. I have been blessed by almost perfect health, and I haven't taken a complete physical since I gave birth to my daughter. I'm not bragging about this, it's just a fact. So when I got this terrible flu, high fever and hacking cough, along with a foot infection that made it almost impossible to walk, my neighbor took me to the ER. My friends, who know my medical preferences, were shocked by my cheerful message on Vicki's answering machine.

Incidentally, several months before I went to the ER, I found a large lump in my left breast. I determined to ignore it, but figured as long as I was there, I'd see what the doctor had to say. He wanted more tests. But no tests for me. Since I'm about to overflow the rim of eighty, I don't choose to live with biopsies, surgeries, tubes sticking out of my body, poisonous injections, nuclear rays shooting through my system, and medication with horrendous side effects in little bottles on my nightstand.

After fifty-plus years of no invasive examinations, it startled me to find myself on a table with my legs raised and my feet in stirrups. I also wondered why I allowed a strange man to feel my lump. My ER experience cemented my desire just to go home and let the Great Physician do what He needs to do.

I invited my adopted daughters over for dinner to tell them about my ER scene and my lump. They accepted my decision to ignore it with various forms of denial. Jennie let out a pathetic, mournful, "Ohhhh." Vicki started to offer advice, and Mary got all teary and immediately prepared for my demise. When I told them my kids were coming to visit, she said, "Are they coming to say good-bye?"

But the gurney ride will always stay in my mind as my best ER memory. While my driver and I sped down the halls to x-ray, I asked, "What's your name?"

"Matthew."

"I like that name. Do you know about Matthew in the Bible?"

"Sure I do. Matthew worked for the IRS, then dumped his job to go fishing."

Over the ensuing days, I began to grow more comfortable with what I'd heard. Maybe not comfortable, really, but peaceful. In *On Golden Pond*, near the end of the movie after the collapse of Henry Fonda's character on the porch, his wife (played by Katharine Hepburn) helps him up to a bench and cradles his head against her chest. She tells him that when she saw him lying on the floor, she thought she'd lost him. Then she says about the thought of death, "[It's] not that bad, really. Not so bad, almost comforting."

There is something to be said about saying hard things right at first so you can get on with it.

That night, talking about lumps—well, you know, it really wasn't so bad. There is something to be said about having things out in the open, something comfortable about beginning a dialogue that will continue till the end, some kind of peace about saying hard things right at first so you can get on with it.

And that lump had been there for a long time. It was a cyst, we all decided. NBD. No big deal.

Nancy came away with more than a holey smile from her dental surgery. Shortly after her ER experience, her back began to hurt more than any of us realized. We speculated that all the yanking that accompanies tooth pulling and her osteoporosis (which I thought we had been ignoring quite successfully for some time) combined to give her a stress fracture in her spine. Nancy didn't comment much about it at first, but it bothered her enough to make another doctor's appointment, which she was again loath to do.

Our relationship entered a new stage with this discovery, and there began a niggling little voice in the back of my head, prodding me to remain alert to her, almost requiring me to ask more frequently about her health, which bugged her. She didn't like to talk about aches and pains. I thought I might be detecting the smallest shadow of fear.

She let me drive her to the doctor for some x-rays. It was like pulling teeth to get her to let me go—and remember, she didn't have many left to pull at that stage—but in the end she let me come, for my sake I'm sure. Again I didn't know what to expect, so I packed up the prerequisite reading material. One should never go anywhere without a book.

She checked in with the front desk, went over her insurance papers, and by the time we'd moved on she *knew* the woman who had helped her, knew her twin girls' names and what church they attended, and had paid two dollars for two fund-raising candy bars. She didn't get a hug before we moved on, but I'm sure only the counter precluded that.

We rode the elevator down to the lower floor, found the office, and after another friendly exchange with a guy behind *that* computer, we settled in the waiting room to people watch, where she told me she was glad I'd come but to keep my mouth shut.

We were feeling our way around this new side of our relationship. She was finding out whether I could be trusted to ferry her about to all these doctors without interfering. I didn't know myself if I could do it.

Just before we went in, I asked her what kind of information, if any, I could request. She permitted me to ask questions as long as I didn't attempt to sway her or the doctor in any particular direction.

After her exam she went to the lab for a chest x-ray with Matthew, the technician from her gurney-with-the-cell-phone expedition. He stood her up against the panels; then he and I scurried behind the wall and he shot the films. He went off to develop them, and Nancy and I talked about mammograms. She had never had one.

"Oh my," I said. "You're missing out."

The doctor came to no conclusions in our presence and sent us home. For the first time in her life, Nancy began taking painkillers, commenting one day as she scooped up a couple of ibuprofen we talked her into, "Isn't it wonderful how well it works?"

It didn't dawn on me to be too concerned about her. She wasn't, or so it seemed. After all, what's a little tiny fracture that didn't slow her down much? It could heal, couldn't it?

It never occurred to me to ask her directly what she thought about all this. Did she suspect there were big changes looming in her future? Did she ever really worry about "looming" things? Maybe she had made it such a habit to be positive that she didn't let herself think about what might be.

Maybe her eyes were not on herself but on us, on me, and how we would handle what she sensed lay ahead.

on holy ground

Two weeks later Nancy moved to the asylum, her pet word for "luxury retirement living."

She called me one night in November, not long after her doctor had confirmed her suspicions about a compression fracture, and left a message on my machine: "I want to talk to you." I called her back right away, but rather than speaking her mind, she set up an appointment for the next morning.

An appointment? In my insecurity I became immediately subdued and wondered through the night if she planned to confront me about something, an issue of my character, something I shouldn't have said, another lesson of some kind. Nothing, absolutely nothing, could have clued me in on what she had to tell me.

She swept through the door enthusiastically the next morning, sat down across from me, and said, "I'm moving."

I didn't understand. "You're moving?"

"Yep," she said. "I'm selling my condo and moving to the Remington Club. Thursday."

We sat there face-to-face, and Nancy began describing the previous twenty-four hours and the huge chain of events she and

God had set in motion . . . they did in one week what would normally take months:

My daily prayer is for God's will, but as searing pain massaged my shoulders, I wondered if my faith in His will would flutter off like a butterfly.

I'd heard about compression fractures from osteoporosis, and instinct warned me that something in my Quasimodo posture had snapped, to change my life in an instant.

X-rays proved my diagnosis. Suddenly, bending over became unacceptable and brought me to the edge of yelling; often I forgot and did it anyway. I bought one of those picker-upper goodies with a handle to squeeze and pinchers at the other end, because I dropped almost everything I touched. Dirty socks wove a path behind me as I headed for my washing machine. Vitamin capsules leaped from my fingers and fled under the bed. Tomatoes rolled out of the refrigerator and snuggled behind the stove. When I opened a bottom drawer to get clean socks, I longed for morphine drops and wished I were in heaven with my husband, but God had another plan. I didn't know how He would orchestrate His plan, but I did know my faith took a front seat on a roller coaster, and I wanted to have a nonstop temper tantrum.

One of my friends looked at me with unflinching blue eyes and uttered an ultimatum. "My mother died of repercussions from osteoporosis. I think you need to move to a care facility while you still can."

I felt squashed and squelched. After she left, I stood looking out at my beautiful view. I longed for my husband and his gentle strength; then I realized I had the Master of gentle strength at my side.

"OK, Lord, I give it all to You. I don't know what to do or where to go. You make the arrangements, and I will stay out of Your way and try to be obedient as You guide me. If I misread Your leading, slam the door in my face."

> *"OK, Lord, You make the arrangements, and I will stay out of Your way and try to be obedient as You guide me."*

I did not tell a soul about my one-way conversation with God. I just sat back and watched Him create His miracles.

I've been known to say I'd rather be run over by an eighteen-wheeler than go to the asylum. God gave me twenty-four hours to get used to the idea that no truck would ram my condo, and then He nudged me to the phone book buried deep in the hall closet. I looked up retirement centers. Tears welled as I dialed the number of the one closest to where I lived. Leslie, a happy-sounding woman, said she'd see me that afternoon at one. God shoved me out the door at noon, so I wouldn't be late, and then His timer started to tick.

Leslie had sleek black hair swept back in an elegant style, and she had a wonderful personality. We liked each other on contact. She had only one one-bedroom apartment available and seemed to apologize for the fact that it was set up for a handicapped tenant. God must have smiled. He knew what I needed.

Though new residents often had to wait for months to move in, this unit would be ready in three days. I paid the first and last months' rent, then Sharon from marketing arrived. She wanted to photocopy my driver's license, and she let out a squeal of surprise when she saw that my maiden name matched the name of the care center.

After Sharon and I did our paperwork, we passed a young lady who looked like my precious granddaughter, Cristina. "Let me introduce you to one of my favorite employees," Sharon said. "This is Christina!" I felt hope seep into my heart.

While I waited to pick up my underground garage opener, I looked at the huge Christmas tree in the lobby. A tiny teddy bear peeked at me from under pine branches, and I thought about Stephanie's teddy. Stephanie lived with me for a year after my husband died. She became one of the sweetest blessings of my life. She and I danced a lot, and her teddy danced with us as our male lead. We'd swing dance and fling him around or cuddle him cheek to cheek during slow dances. She'd had her teddy almost twenty-five years, and of course took him with her when she went off to marry her darling. I missed her beautiful spirit and teddy's tolerant acceptance of our silliness.

I shook away my reverie and thanked Sharon for my garage opener and all her help, then I started out the front door. A sinking feeling embraced me. Grief wrapped around me, and I wanted to wail. My independence went through the door with me and raced away across the parking lot. *Are You certain You want me in this place, Lord?*

He didn't answer, and I stood there longing to get on my knees. Wanting to beg Him for another sign that He really wanted me here.

Sharon called to me, "Nancy, take a copy of our December newsletter with you."

I looked at it, stunned. Stephanie's teddy had his picture on the cover. Same seams stitched down his tummy. Same perky ears. Same pads on his feet. He had on a Christmas hat and a Christmas package in his paws. The tears I'd stifled ran down my cheeks and made wet spots on his picture. *OK, Lord. OK. I'm sure now this is where You want me.*

> "I've decided to let God manage all my decisions. Forever and ever. Amen."

The next morning, twenty-four hours after I'd begun this process, I phoned a real-estate broker who went to my church. "Tom, I want to sell my condo. How soon can you look at it?"

"Is an hour soon enough?" he asked.

Then I called Pampered Packing. The owner packed and

unpacked and had movers to work with her. She said she would help me but couldn't do it for another week or so and her movers were all booked up too. I hung up and had just started to pout when my phone rang. "The movers had a cancellation on Thursday, and I was able to change my Thursday job, so we'll be at your condo at 8:00 that morning."

God continued to move at top speed, and I apologized for pouting.

I slept in my new apartment on Thursday night. On Saturday afternoon Tom, my broker, called. "I just sold your condo to a couple in my Bible study."

So in six days God put it together, just like He did when He made heaven and earth.

I've decided to let Him manage all my decisions. Forever and ever. Amen.

As we talked that morning, I felt relief on three counts: first that I hadn't said anything to hurt her; second, that God had obviously had a hand in all the many details that came together in record time; and third, that she'd made this very difficult decision. After all, she had said to us earlier, tongue in cheek, what if she fell and broke her hip and starved to death.

Vicki, Jennie, and I had already had a few clandestine conversations about her safety living alone in her condo. But we were clueless to the fact that we were on the verge of making decisions for a woman who was completely capable of figuring out her own life. We meant well, of course, but we chickened out when it came to talking openly about our concerns. Thankfully, Nancy took matters into her own hands, and what she chose ended up being the best for everyone.

Not long after, before she had to, she gave up driving. She donated Peppermint, her green Dodge with the dove on the bumper, to the church for the staff to use when they needed extra wheels. Saying good-bye to that car she loved enough to name, and with it her freedom to come and go as she pleased, was not easy.

For all Nancy's appreciation of the spontaneous, she did like control. These plans she made so quickly and decisively took her out from under anyone's influence, except for God's and she had no problem with Him. Looking back, I am so glad we three girls weren't the ones to get her moving.

It was comforting to all of us to know that help would now be a button-click away, comforting to get Nancy out of her condo where her upstairs neighbors had not always been savory types, comforting also to see her continue to take responsibility for her life. But the thought that she'd gone ahead and placed herself in a retirement center—what she had, without affection, called "the asylum" all these years—stunned us. And the realization that she'd had the idea, considered and prayed about it, and acted upon it in the space of one day—without any of us even suspecting!—took our breath away.

It was a total act of faith, reminiscent of her quick response to Lynn when he would crook his finger for her to follow. Except this time she went where she didn't want to go. Yet there was no kicking and screaming, no pity party, no second-guessing.

We supported her decision, of course, not that our disapproval would have kept her from moving. (She probably didn't tell us for fear we'd slow her down.) Yet we also mourned with her over the necessity of it. We just didn't think she'd ever get to this point. Perhaps we thought, naively, her positive attitude would be enough to keep her healthy.

When moving day arrived, I packed my Jeep with small stuff—some of the wonderful driftwood she'd collected over the years, boxes of loose things we'd wrested from the giveaway piles ("Nance, you have to keep at least two bowls!")—and ferried Nancy's treasures from the condo where she and Lynn shared their last days to her new digs in the Remington Club.

Her old condo gave her sunsets; her new place gleamed with the neon lights of the neighborhood supermarket's loading docks. Even so, if you sat on the couch in the morning and looked out the window at just the right angle, all you saw were trees and grass and the neat little neighboring apartments. It was a pretty view from that vantage point and a great little place—light, snug, yet roomy.

Her first night there, our pastor, Ray (Vicki's husband and Nancy's surrogate son), prayed a prayer of dedication and protection. With all the confluence of details, it didn't take much to convince us we were standing on holy ground.

She went from two bedrooms, two baths, to one of each. Everything she kept just fit. Her furniture tucked in like the accoutrement in a Pullman train car—and she did love trains. All the kitchen cabinets were low, built for wheelchair users, much better for Nancy's height because they kept her from having to reach. The sink was so low, I could have done dishes on my knees, and Nancy could work there from a chair if she wanted.

The walls were pinky salmon colored. We didn't like it at first, but they threw a healthy glow on all of us that was a nice perk we hadn't expected.

But the best feature, when all was said and done, was the private outside entrance that most of the apartments did not have. Friends would stop nearby to pick up their cleaning or get a cup of coffee or a haircut and swing by Nancy's on their way home. My son, Matt, drove by frequently, and honked and hooted and hollered if he couldn't stop, tickled by the fact he was buzzing a retirement center.

One Sunday soon after she moved in, she counted thirty-two visitors. What a spectacle we made, traipsing in and out at all hours of the day and night. It was an unexpected blessing to be unrestricted and often undetected, and not have to sign in at the front desk.

Plus, this way we could pretend she wasn't really there.

Lumping herself in with the elderly set had never felt right to Nancy. So when she finally made the move to her new home, it seemed to take awhile before she was able to accept her new neighborhood . . . and her neighbors. She met a rather snooty resident her first day and described him as having "the kind of eyes you want to stick a fork into."

She made friends with the staff right away—the ladies who came to clean, the gardeners and janitors, the guy who came several times to get rid of the pesky ants in her kitchen.

> *She met a rather snooty resident and described him as having "the kind of eyes you want to stick a fork into."*

And it didn't take long for her to hear some of the residents' stories—stories of people just like her, adventurous world travelers who were willing to put up with anything to go somewhere they really wanted to see. Even her rebuff in the dining room (when the maître d' tried to sit her with an established patron who said in her hearing, "Why would I want to sit with her? *I don't even know her!*") wasn't enough to discourage her from wanting to make friends, to discover as much about them as she had about us.

Off we went one day to Wal-Mart to find the things one always has to find to finish the settling-in process. Cleaning stuff, a longer, heavier shower curtain, a microwave. Nancy was feeling pretty good, except for the growing pain in her back, but she didn't have a lot of stamina.

Inside the door we happened upon Wal-Mart's motorized shopping carts. Just for the fun of it—or maybe not—she let the resident senior show her how to work one, and her eyes lit up with a feisty glint as she tore off down the aisles, maneuvering between other shoppers and an occasional post like a four-year-old on a new tricycle. She didn't say a word, but I knew she was determined not to act like a little old lady with health problems, even though she looked like—and was—one.

I piled our purchases in her cart and balanced the microwave on top of the basket until she could barely see. On a whim we picked up a disposable camera to record the moment . . . which we lost within a week.

Doing the practical things was a relief. I didn't want the dubious luxury of time to contemplate all I was seeing, to sit around and speculate on the future. I didn't want to just pray for her either. I wanted to fix it.

Finding the right shower curtain would have to do.

what a difference
a week makes

Nancy's compression fracture proved to be the least of her problems. The real culprit was that wily lump in her breast that we all preferred to ignore. Rather than let her do that, it seemed to have gone off on a little foray, depositing deadly fingers in otherwise healthy places. We found out that, though the fracture was painful and definitely present, the mass that had formed around her spinal column was what was causing the most severe pain. In mid-January, just weeks after she moved to the Remington Club, an MRI brought the mass and the future to light: metastasized breast cancer.

I knew the pain was becoming intolerable when I stopped by one January morning to get a prescription she needed filled and watched her grimace as she rose from the couch. The next day I left for five days in Florida; when I returned she had progressed to round-the-clock morphine. We immediately set up a schedule to ensure that someone who loved her would be there all the time. What a difference a week makes.

I went by the morning after my trip to see for myself how she was. As I suspected would be true, the apartment teemed with visitors. Nancy sat in a comfortable chair, thin, a little wan, loving the attention, occasionally losing track of the conversation. That night I returned at 7:00 to spend the night and the next day, not sure of what I'd find, and a little frightened of the hours ahead of me. But the earlier days of adjustment to her medication while I'd been gone peaked that night and everything went well—so well, in fact, that the next day we worked on our book for three hours.

That rapid change in her health jolted us from our relaxed work schedule and the feeling that we could take as long as we wanted to finish. Now our self-imposed deadlines were on the forefront of our minds, and we were scrambling to pull out all the good stuff while we could. I've faced deadlines before, but never with such a cloud following me around.

I was full of wishful thoughts: *I wish we'd worked harder in the fall when we had lots of time and plenty of good health. I wish I were better at organization so we could see clearly where this book was going and, therefore, what it would take to get it there. I wish we didn't even have to address these issues of pain and morphine. How can we keep our focus on life when death is so loud?*

I read the above to Nancy and she piped up with, "We can keep our focus, Mary, because life is so much more powerful than death! Life is full of flowers blooming and babies' red cheeks and sweet stuff." I scribbled fast to get it all down.

Nancy had my mother's hands, something I've not found in anyone else. I noticed it one day and picked her hand up out of her lap, held it in mine; turned it over, feeling its feel, and said aloud, surprised, "You have my mother's hands."

My mother died in 1990 when I was forty years old. Even when it's the right time—and we can sometimes know that—losing a mother changes so many aspects of our lives. As the firstborn of three sisters, my mother's death made me the matriarch of our immediate family, a role I didn't want and felt ill-prepared to take. I might have been prepared if my mother were around to teach me.

Of course, it's not the role but the loss of *her* that makes it difficult. We were the closest of friends. People stopped us on the street to comment on our physical resemblance, having no idea that we were alike in so many other ways. We laughed at the same jokes and had similar opinions about the world. Once I became a Christian and could put it into words, we had our faith to share. And around us like a big bubble was a familiar "comfortability" that she expressed to me in precious words one morning shortly before she died: "Honey, being around you is like slipping on a comfortable old shoe."

How can we keep our focus on life when death is so loud?

Her battle with non-Hodgkins lymphoma was a difficult period for all of us. My two sisters shouldered most of the care since I lived two states away with young children and a traveling husband. I know I have only limited understanding of all they went through.

It dawned on me that morning, looking at Nancy's hands, that maybe I had been refusing to acknowledge the mother/daughter aspect of our relationship. I guess it's not so surprising I didn't notice it before because, once I had gotten to know her, I always felt that Nancy was my peer and not my mother.

But if a mother is one who loves you, who's interested in the trivial details of your life, who cares what you look like but doesn't care at the same time, who doesn't let you get away with negative thinking and calls you on stuff, I'll have to admit she did play that role. For me, for Vicki and Jennie, and for countless others.

Nancy formed a deep bond with Matt and Molly as she did with Jennie's and Vicki's children. She wanted to know the kinds of things grandmothers want to know, about how school was going, who their friends were, what they were likely to choose as hobbies and extracurricular activities, how they were feeling about life. She would get them alone and make them open up and own up, listening patiently, offering advice, prodding them to make better choices, slipping them some cash, and not telling us a thing about it.

But we'd see them together and suspect what was going on.

There was never any question about where her real allegiances lay: her children, Lynn's children, and all the "grands."

Nancy told me about the time she and Johnny were on a commuter train, he a two-year-old and she worn out from reading the same story over and over and over. Johnny took his book and wandered off down the car. Nancy watched as he found a man who took him on his knee and read the story one more time. It was Spencer Tracy.

One day she regaled me with stories about Kathy's wedding in Spain, about sewing her wedding dress and how one night she sewed Kathy *into* the dress, between the lining and the top layer, and what a hilarious time they had trying to get her out without destroying anything. About how Kathy's new husband knew only a few words of English. Motivated by devotion, he memorized one English song to sing for her in the limo as they left the church— "Please release me, let me go, for I don't love you anymore."

She talked on and on about Cristina, Kathy's daughter in whom Nancy saw herself, and kept us up-to-date on her work as a hair stylist to some of the big Hollywood names, as a clothes designer of sought-after hip couture, as a wild child who called her Nani. They had a unique bond that went beyond blood to spirit.

With Nancy's move and admission that her health would now be an issue, we began to see more of Kathy and Cristina. They'd come separately or together, from different parts of California, and bunk down on Nancy's couch. Johnny made several trips from his home in Hawaii. When they were around, we did our best to let them be the family. We wondered how they felt about us but didn't know how to ask.

As things grew more serious, though, our communication increased, and little by little we got to know Nancy's family the way people going through big things together get to know one another. In the end we were a unit, all doing whatever we could to make her comfortable and meet her needs. Between us all we could cover a lot of ground.

Though Nancy's family shared her wanderlust and her love, she knew they didn't share her faith. Since she was so invested in her children, it broke her heart. Day after day her sense of urgency grew that they would know the width, breadth, and depth of her relationship with God. And she knew she couldn't keep telling them. They had to see it in her life. But with all she was going through, it wasn't easy.

One day I walked into her place to find her strangely agitated, in fact, more bothered than I had ever seen her. Molly was there and our friend Judy. I found them in very concentrated prayer. Nancy pulled me down beside her right away and handed me a handwritten note she'd received just that day from the director of the Remington Club, a casual but personal friend. "Nancy," he'd said in effect, "we've noticed that you haven't been eating in the dining room. Is there anything we can do to better accommodate your dietary needs?"

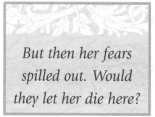

But then her fears spilled out. Would they let her die here?

I thought, *What a nice note! How kind of him to notice and how thoughtful of him to write.*

Nancy was always up for eating out, yet she didn't often eat in the dining room, even though her new housing situation provided meals. (I can attest to the fact that the food was what you'd expect from a very nice, but true to form, retirement center—soft.) Nancy was accustomed to natural foods and a healthy diet, and she had an established regimen that was easier to follow in her own little kitchen. Plus, she ate little and quickly, and it didn't seem worth the bother to walk all the way to the dining room, even when she could.

I took the note, read it again, and looked in her face. And suddenly I realized she was afraid.

First, she swore us to secrecy and made me promise not to breathe a word of the note to anybody, even Vicki and Jennie for some reason. Then she read the note aloud again, slowly, searching for any nuance she might have missed earlier. I couldn't figure out why she was taking this so hard. It seemed perfectly innocuous to me.

But then her fears spilled out. She worried that the staff was taking notice of her illness and marking each time her friend Ruth, the home-healthcare nurse, came in and out. She dreaded the idea of being moved from her independent living situation to the assisted living wing, which she'd already inspected and rejected outright. Would she have to leave this perfect setup, where her dearest friends could pop over with so little trouble, where she had privacy and, more important, control? Would they let her die here?

So we added another discussion on attitude and fear to our portfolio. Only this time Nancy was the focus. It was a little disconcerting. But, of course, I understood completely where she was coming from.

Still, I missed the twinkle in her eye, the sparkle that assured me the world is good, things would work out, and with God in charge there was no need to be afraid. There was a perverse part of me that wanted to say, "Aha! Gotcha!" But even in the midst of such thoughts, I knew I'd rather have her old self than a reflection of me.

"Are you afraid?" I asked her.

"Funny, I don't think of it as fear," she said, her eyes betraying her.

It seemed like a cop-out. But after all, she was dying. What could I say?

Kathy and Cristina were in her face though. The two women she loved most in the world, the two she wanted to prove God to. They challenged her. Where is your faith? they asked. Show us your faith.

I wanted the same thing.

We shared a faith, Nancy and I. It was an understood assumption we lived with, like the sun coming up in the morning. I knew where she stood, and she knew where I stood.

Occasionally I would read the psalms to her, or we'd pray for a specific need, or one of us would have heard something interesting and bring it up, or we'd hear a praise song and we'd sing along with it. I knew she was praying and reading her large-print Bible, which she kept open in her living room to Zephaniah 3:17, "The LORD your God is with you, he is mighty to save. He will take great delight in you, he will quiet you with his love, he will rejoice over you with singing." Every phrase in the verse had meaning for her.

Because she had cultivated such a close relationship with God through all kinds of situations, she knew how to get to Him. But even with the strength of her beliefs and her determination to be optimistic, she had days of fear and sadness. Illness does that to us. Those days kept her ever vigilant for evidences of God, because positive thinking can't wipe out pain. And in a small way these glimpses of weakness added dimension to her personality, like in good fiction where the hero leaves his dirty socks all over the house and the villain is a scoundrel but loves his mother.

So where was her faith? It was tucked inside the covers with her in the middle of the night when she tried to sleep yet couldn't turn off her mind or her pain. It was spread around her when she sat in her chair and held court with family and friends. It hovered over her, like that good old sun outside the window, even when she wondered if she could carry on.

It was captured in the note she stuck on the fridge: "Perks to having the 'Big C'—no bra ☺, no shoes, friends friends friends, blessings blessings blessings!"

"How is your spiritual life?" I asked her one good day. "Tell me what you see."

"I'm overwhelmed with the Lord's presence," she said with a smile. "I see Him everywhere. I see Him in the little man who changed the light bulb just now and cared enough about my bathing habits to go in and fix my shower."

like the setting sun

There on the couch in Nancy's snug little apartment with the pink walls, I spent the night now and then, taking turns with her many friends in keeping her company around the clock. You could get a pretty good sleep if you took the back cushions off the couch before you laid out your sleeping bag, and remembered to turn off the chimes on the ship's clock that announced the half hours.

She was a night owl. I would read in the living room for a while, turn off the light, and hear her rustling papers. When they finally dropped from her hands and hit the floor, I'd know she was asleep. It would be midnight. We'd sleep until my alarm rang at 2 a.m., when I woke her to take a tiny white morphine pill to keep the level of medication constant and her screaming pain manageable.

One morning I knelt by her bed and put my head on her lap. She stroked my hair, and we had a discussion I thought would be further down the line. She told me she was wondering more and more about how this would all end, how much pain she would have to face, and if it would make her cry out. She was very aware of the young girls who cared about her and shared companionship duties, particularly Jennie's younger girls, Katie and Lissie. She knew they wanted to be around her ("Katie's like a little sticker right here," she said, patting her shoulder), but she didn't want them exposed to anything that might scare them.

Ruth the nurse came over that day. Nancy had to have a catheter. She was not thrilled with the prospect but stoic about it, submitting to Ruth's medical expertise and kind hands and heart.

"I was thinking you always seem so proper and so just right," she said to me later. "And so I felt really protective of you at that moment. You wanted to come in and hold my hand while I was getting a treatment I've never had before, and I didn't know if I was going to yell. It's like I wanted to tie a bandanna over your eyes so you couldn't see it, and shove earplugs in your ears so you couldn't hear it."

Out of deference, and obedience, I left the room. But I couldn't stay away. It seemed important to be with her, holding her hand, being some kind of diversion. So I went back in and sat next to her bed, holding that hand of hers that was so like my mother's. It wasn't enough to just sit there though. And, for some reason, it didn't seem like prayer would be enough either. I realized we needed to sing.

"Suddenly in the midst of all this," she remembered, "you—this one we think of as kind of fragile—started singing 'Onward Christian Soldiers.' So I joined in . . . and it was so right. It must have been the Lord. It has great words; it gave us hope and strength. And whenever we hear this song again, you and I, we'll have this little kind of smug contentment, a little shared memory . . ."

Oh, brother.

Vicki, Jennie, dozens of other friends, and I had roles to play in this drama. And with all of us, it looked more than a little like a grand old block party. We'd run into old friends we hadn't talked to in months, measure their growing children, and catch up on details. Some did errands, hung curtain rods, put up shelving. Some cooked, baked, or kept the pecans, Gouda, and chocolate in stock. Some supplied the apartment with fresh flowers; some came to play the keyboard and sing. Some provided the medical care. Some came to pray. Molly brought over her guitar a few times. Carla brought movies. (Nancy had a thing for actor Hector Elizondo and the movie *Tortilla Soup*. She played it over and over and over.) Jennie's daughter, Jordan, brought her baby, Micah, over every day. Nancy would take his little hand and ask for a dance.

And Ronda, the creative, competent seamstress, figured out a clever sleeve to hide Esmerelda, the catheter tube. It was the one vestige of helplessness Nancy couldn't bear to expose.

As Nancy's health began to deteriorate, I fell into a mode of thinking of which I'm not very proud. I began to grow impatient with her refusal to discuss moving to the assisted-living wing of her complex. I never saw it and can't attest to its suitability, but I will admit to frustration as I watched her growing need for expert care, and saw all of us trying to meet her medical needs as well as being there as companions twenty-four hours a day. I spouted off more than once to Jennie and Vicki, and I'm sure I made them very uncomfortable.

In fact, we went to see a play—reportedly a comedy—about an older woman, her daughter, and her home-healthcare nurse. I thought it would be a kick and that we'd relate to the characters and have a night of laughter and sweet recognition.

It wasn't quite like that, however. This triangle wasn't such a happy one. In the drama the older woman saw her autonomy falling away, the daughter didn't have the time to see it happening and to recognize that she was the instigator, and the nurse was summarily dismissed when the daughter saw that her mother had grown attached to her. This play left me identifying

> *I saw how my desire to wrap things up in neat packages can sometimes ignore the complexity of human beings.*

with the insensitive daughter, and it made me feel ashamed. I saw how my desire to wrap things up in neat packages can sometimes ignore the complexity of situations, and even more so, the complexity of human beings. It's so easy to minimize the fierce struggle elderly people go through balancing autonomy and dependency.

I read a personal essay titled "My Grandmother, the Bag Lady." The author described retrieving her grandmother's purse from the other room and finding it unexpectedly heavy. She peeked and poked inside and discovered what was left of all her grandmother's favorite things, the last remnants of her life. Everything else had been slowly stripped away.

I realized I was naive to think a decision could be made with little or no wrestling, that it wouldn't be a big deal for Nancy to give up this next bit of independence. I am embarrassed to admit that I was so eager to make things neat that I almost missed *her*.

And that became another lesson: *don't allow the practical matters to get in the way of the person.*

Another "fact of the aging life" that the play brought to our attention was the completely unrealistic scene being played out at Nancy's day after day after day. I couldn't believe the numbers and variety of well-wishers (what a clumsy term for such affection) that attended her. Though I knew most of them, others seemed to appear from some corner of her life that we had never heard about. They all wanted to spend time with her, wanted to *waste* time with her. It never let up.

She was just as puzzled as I.

"I never would have dreamt," she said, "that I could be sitting in my little apartment behind the Vons loading dock, welcoming so many visitors. I really can't understand it. Are they coming because I'm a friend of the pastor or because it seems like the right thing to do? I have no idea," she said with her typical shoulder shrug.

"And they don't come just once," I said. "They come again and again . . . and it's not like they're coming to say their last good-byes."

"Yes!" she said. "When they come it's fun! Were you here when Kathy and Gary put their eyebrows on?"

like the setting sun

She never did fully understand. Vicki, Jennie, and I talked it over more than once. I suppose when someone seems so alive, so interested in you, so vested in what matters to you, that you come to pay homage, to mend breaches, to comfort, to console, perhaps to catch one last glimpse before your friend slips into eternity. Or sometimes you come just to be loved for a few more minutes.

We reflected on the sad contrast with other residents of the place, some who wandered the hallways, lonely, wistfully looking for a visitor, sometimes even peeking longingly into Nancy's partylike room when the hall door was left ajar.

"You're just not the usual 'older' friend," I told her once. "I think most people desire to connect with the older generation . . . but they're a little afraid because they don't know how. Will they have anything in common? Is it going to mean a huge responsibility? All giving and no getting?"

She jumped on that one. "We've had a give-and-take relationship always, all four of us have, but from now on there's not going to be any giving on my part, I don't think. The burden's going to lie on you guys."

"But the interesting thing is," I said, "that if you really get down to the bottom of it, what you've given us all along is the same thing you give us now. It's your mind and your conversation, your head and your heart."

"*Now* I know I'm a burden," Nancy said to me one day, as I was typing her answers to some questions into my computer. I shifted

133

my focus to this topic and made her speak slowly enough so I wouldn't miss a word.

"I'm no longer the fun person you'd pop in the car and off we'd go with our snacks and our books and our minds on learning. Suddenly I'm a burden and a responsibility. And you're stuck with it."

"How does it make you feel?" I asked her.

"Nothing I can do about it, you know. I'm grateful that you're here, grateful that it's you. I just count my blessings and am in complete shock at the response to my being ill. But, our relationship, yours with me, is so different all of a sudden. Is the joy gone?"

"No, of course not. It doesn't even feel that different to me," I said. "It might get difficult if you ever got to the place where you wouldn't take our advice or you didn't trust us, or you got paranoid and were afraid of us. But it sort of seems like the natural course of events. It doesn't feel burdensome, maybe because we'd developed this friendship to start with and we're working on the book and need to be together anyway. I don't really mind it for some reason."

"That's great," she said, "because of the three of you, I would think that you'd mind it the most."

"You would?"

"You'd be the most uncomfortable, out of your element with it. But obviously you're not; you're hanging in there well."

"I guess it just comes out of you when you have to do something."

"I'm trying to separate all this into little segments in my mind," she said, "so that I'll get away from the overwhelming responsibility that you girls have taken on for me. Knowing full well that I could go hire a nurse—I can afford it—yet feeling in myself the need for that little touch that means it's *you*. I may lose consciousness, become paralyzed—then is the time for nurses. But now you all can come over; we can have fun and giggle. In my mind it's a time to be blessed, you all to bless me and me to bless you. I still think we have something profound to offer one another. When the day comes that we don't, we can move on to the next step. And between us we'll know."

We did know, finally. After four months of constant companionship from one of us, Kathy, Johnny, or Cristina, or one of the myriad friends who made themselves available, one night we had to welcome a stranger into our circle of immediate friends. The time had come for overnight home healthcare. Nancy was *not* happy about it. She had grown accustomed to our faces. We were dear to her, familiar and safe. She knew how we'd react and had discovered that we could handle what she was going through without histrionics. All day long I knew she was dreading the entrance of this new person who would be her all-night companion. Change is hard, particularly when it signals a downturn in your health and the arrival of the unfamiliar. Especially a stranger.

The doorbell rang at 9:00 p.m. I rushed to open it, with a few knowing looks at Jennie and Vicki, and in walked Virginia, smiling already. Her smile broadened when she caught Nancy's eye. Somewhere she'd seen her before, Virginia exclaimed. "I know you!" She walked over to Nancy and took her hand and looked at her warmly. What a relief.

Virginia, Yvonne, Carmen. One by one the Lord brought these caring, competent, patient women into all our lives. About one Nancy said, "We're a good team. The things that drive me crazy drive her crazy. She understands why I want to get things organized and feels exactly the same way. I wake up to such pain that is just intolerable and she's there. She's just right, not overly inquisitive, not overly solicitous, she's just right, like in 'The Three Bears.'"

In the middle of all this upheaval, we wrote. Every day we talked and every other day, it seemed, I'd trundle over with my laptop, and we'd try, in our convoluted, easily distractible way, to come up with something new and printable. Oh, but it was hard! We would collapse in giggles at the slightest provocation, and we were way too welcoming of all the visitors and phone calls.

Rebecca made us a sign to post on the gate. One side said, "Welcome, Friends." The other said, "Writers at Work—Please Call Again." It was the perfect solution to many of the interruptions, only we could see her visitors through the blinds walking up the path and didn't have the heart to turn them away, except very occasionally when we were really on a roll.

Nancy's eyes were like the setting sun as time went on. The sun lay down and her eyes closed, and you couldn't stop either one.

like the setting sun

Those days when I took my computer to her apartment to do some writing, I was never sure what I would find. Some days she was talkative and up and down, folding towels, fixing a snack; other days she was in a constant state of drowse, her head dropping to her chest in the middle of dialing the phone, or the moment after she'd asked me to read to her.

Nancy's eyes were like the setting sun. The sun lay down and her eyes closed, and you couldn't stop either one.

When she was awake and cheerful, she handed me wonderful lines I typed up on my laptop. Together we would giggle our way through another paragraph. I continued to marvel at her creativity and wondered why I ever despaired of finishing our book. Other times I resigned myself to the fact that I would have to write her stories from now on, that she would only be able to listen and nod. But then she'd surprise me again and off we'd go.

In mid-February I called Nancy from Pennsylvania, where I'd gone for a few days—to Hershey, the chocolate capital. I had just been gone a day or two, and I was surprised by the hoarseness in her voice. She had been sounding weaker each time we talked, and this time she told me she wanted to finish this book by the end of the week when I got home. I laughed out loud over the cell phone, thinking, grasping, that she was just kidding, but then I wondered exactly what she was saying to me. She told me she'd been writing small snippets for the book, that I'd be pleased when we got together to look at it all. She thought we had reams of excellent material. I wanted to look at it with the same positive attitude, but I couldn't. Reality is reality. Of course, I didn't want to tell her *that*.

Expectations were so high though. High all around. Friends and almost-strangers asked us repeatedly how the writing was going. Nancy's life was so legendary and her stories, or the rumor of them, were so anticipated that everyone wanted a peek.

Yet as I continued to draw our material together, I found that her stories were getting pushed aside by her dying. At first it was troublesome. Then, finally, it *was* the story.

in the midst of living

Someone once told Nancy the last thing she'd do before she died is pick up lint off the throw rugs. I believed it. When I spent the night with her those early spring days, before I left I'd fluff those throw rugs, do a final sweep with Windex on the glass coffee table, and spritz a little vanilla scent in the air, all under her watchful eye. She liked things neat, orderly, and sweet smelling, never with a hint that it might be a sickroom.

You wouldn't have known it was a sickroom by what was going on around her. Fresh daffodils just opening grew in a pot on the coffee table. The early spring breeze blew the last of the winter-dead leaves through the open door—and with them countless visitors. It was really too small a place to entertain so many, but no one seemed to mind.

One day when Nancy had dozed off and it was that lazy time of the afternoon when your lunch makes you sleepy and you need a short power nap and it's warm yet breezy, I stretched out on her couch for a few quiet minutes. There were a lot of other things going on in my life and family at the time, and I didn't often have downtime. I wanted to sleep for a few minutes, but it was just so pleasant I wanted to stay awake too. So I lay there and looked back over the previous weeks, making a mental note of all the people who had stopped by. That afternoon I began to ask myself some hard questions that continue to haunt me in a gentle way.

Who will pop in to see me when I'm dying? Will my sickroom be a gathering place for friends? Will anyone consider it *fun* to visit me at that time of my life? Will I remember that vanilla-scent spritz trick?

Dying goes on right in the midst of living. How nice it would be to order everything, to set it up as in a play, with everything rehearsed and going according to plan. Sometimes that happens, I hear; sometimes the loved ones are gathered, the arrangements made, the refrigerator full for the guests. The dying one is peace-filled and sweet smelling, and it's the middle of the afternoon so no one loses more sleep.

Why, in most cases though, is it *not* smooth? Why, when we know death for the Christian means merely passing from one life to the next—and we're looking forward to the next—why is it so unpleasant? Why has God allowed this stage of life to be such a chore?

A week before Nancy died, when her legs were paralyzed and she sat in her bed day after day, she had one of those mornings I'm sure she's going over and over with her friends in heaven to this day. Or maybe not.

It didn't begin as a day to talk about. She woke in a torrent of diarrhea, and by the time the nurse got to her, it had worked its way up her back and all over. Jennie's teenage daughter, Katie, was there, as was Johnny, but Nancy cringed at the thought that Katie and Johnny had to deal with the mess at all, so she called Jennie to ask her to come and be one more woman-presence. I don't think she thought I could handle it.

Such a disaster could not happen on this of all days. Jerry Jenkins and his wife, Dianna, were on their way from Colorado Springs for one thing only, to visit Nancy before she died. And she wanted to be ready early.

Jerry called Nancy "Tess." When they met in 1990 at a writers' conference, he was already a respected and successful author. Nancy made an appointment with him to look at a manuscript she was working on. He helped her get published in

Who will pop in to see me when I'm dying? Will my sickroom be a gathering place for friends?

Moody Monthly (later *Moody Magazine*), where he was editor, and they became fast friends, visiting each other when possible and keeping in touch by letter and, later, e-mail.

One day in 1995 Jerry sent her a book manuscript, as he often did after their friendship and mutual respect as writers were established. She relished getting a first look at his stuff, and she wrote him a note saying, "It'll be a *New York Times* bestseller. I'm sure of it." The manuscript was titled *Left Behind*.

Jerry was used to her cheerleading, but when the book later hit the top of every bestseller list and its sequels became the best-selling books on the planet, he began to call her his prophetess, which she shortened to "Tess" and used as her sign-off to him from then on.

Nancy adored Jerry and Dianna and didn't want to make them uncomfortable in her tiny room that morning. Jennie, Katie, and the nurse bathed her, cleaned the mess, changed the sheets, opened the windows, spritzed that vanilla scent, and fussed around her with enough flurry to calm her and communicate that they knew what this day meant to her. She wanted her hair combed just so, and she picked out her blouse with as much excitement as if she had a date to the prom. She wanted the blankets and bedspread draped in a certain way, the curtain pulled back to let in sunlight and air, and the room spritzed again and again. As the finishing touch, she called and begged me to hurry over with some makeup. She dabbed it on her chin and sent me off.

And then they arrived. Hugs, sweet smiles, glistening eyes, choked voices. Everyone but Jennie (who had been asked to stay and who described this morning to me) dismissed themselves, giving Nancy, Jerry, and Dianna private time together. Jerry held her hand, made a few jokes, and videotaped an interview with her for an upcoming conference. Then he read her Psalm 91. He read with emotion and such caring, the words washing over Nancy as she sat there, eyes watching him, taking in their faces, hearing those precious words, drinking them in as they soothed her soul. His voice broke as he read, "He shall give His angels charge over you, to keep you . . ."

The sweet, short time ended with farewells, hugs, tears, and Nancy waving wistfully through the window as they crossed through the yard. Dianna turned to give Nancy one last tearful smile, and Jerry called out he loved her. Nancy turned to Jennie and said, "My writing career just came full circle. It began with Jerry. It ended today."

Had we finished the book together, this is the dedication Nancy had chosen: "To my master mentor, Jerry B. Jenkins, and in memory of my master husband, Lynn M. Bayless."

The Jenkinses' visit signaled the last round of good-byes. I remember that day. Joe was there. Faithful Joe. He would show up from time to time from who-knows-where. We spoke briefly when I brought my makeup over, and when I left, I saw him sitting alone in the corner of the living room while Jerry, Dianna, and Nancy visited in private. For years and years Joe had been a steadying presence in Nancy's life, helping her start anew after her hard first marriage, quietly appearing at her side during the difficult years when Lynn was sick, and now holding his own little vigil at her bedside as she lay dying.

"I can't imagine a world without Nancy," he said once during those final days, and we all wondered what it was that held him to her for so many years. I wish we'd asked.

Lynn's family trickled in for short visits; Johnny came and bunked in for a long week; Kathy racked up more miles flying from northern California. Cristina came anytime she could get away.

Matt called from Scotland, where he was in school. He carried most of the conversation, getting occasional murmurs from

Nancy's end of the line. He told me how strange it was to be so removed from, yet so connected to, the life-and-death matters that were going on around his family.

Old friends of Nancy's would call to chat or show up at the door. She never wanted the focus on herself (though once while I was there she talked to someone on the phone who didn't even ask how she was, and she made a comment on that, this dying woman). Always she wanted the pervading mood to be one of joy and laughter, of light and vanilla, of common and interesting conversation.

Maybe I was the only one who didn't realize that those last days as we massaged Nancy's feet she probably couldn't feel it. She lay there and loved us as we loved her, and she didn't say a thing to discourage our tender loving care. Even in dying, even with morphine, she had our best interests at heart and kept on encouraging us.

She made it awfully easy to be with her.

I found myself very stoic—way too stoic—as I watched Nancy dying. Once I told her, when she wondered out loud if I was getting anything from this experience, that in one very real sense this was an opportunity to do for her what I was not near enough to do for my own mother. She accepted that, and I'm sure my mom in heaven was equally accepting. Still, as involved as I was, I felt removed, as if I was holding back that emotion that should flood us when we're part of something so big with someone so important. I will admit to some guilt over that . . . and I know Nancy is shaking her finger at me right this minute as I type.

A week before she died, I had to wrestle with a difficult decision. Molly and I were scheduled to leave for a trip to Scotland and Ireland, part business, part pleasure. As the day of departure grew closer, my anxiety grew. Maybe I should send Molly on ahead and meet up with her in Ireland; that would save a week. Maybe I should give up my responsibilities at the conference we were attending. Not that big a deal. But what was right? Was there a right answer?

I spent the morning in tears. An out-of-town friend phoned out of the blue and, at my request, prayed for my decision with such detail and pathos, I cried even more. I called Jennie to talk it out, crying still, and she asked me if I was concerned about what people would say were I not there when Nancy died or later at her service. I thought about it for a while and realized that was not my problem. I'd spent a great deal of time with Nancy—I could, after all, with my children grown and my responsibilities light. Then I realized I was concerned about letting her down, abandoning her at her most neediest time. Possibly even running away. Maybe protecting myself.

I knew that if Nancy knew I was wrestling with all this, she would laugh and say, "Go!" So, though I could have, I didn't remind her that my trip was coming up. I didn't really want her to have any say in my decision, and though she was lucid much of the time, it didn't seem to be anything she needed to deal with.

Later that day I went over and laid it all on Kathy. She laughed just like her mother would have and said, "Go! This is just the kind of self-defeating attitude Mom's been trying to get out of you all this time!"

So I began packing, spending as much time as I could with Nancy, kneeling by her bed, sitting at her feet, stroking her arms, letting her stroke me, praying with her, hovering. Kathy and Johnny, and Vicki, Jennie, and I, took turns walking to the grocery store, picking up Starbucks, getting salads and fish tacos at Baja Fresh, all just steps from her door. We kept careful watch over medications, made what decisions we could to ensure her greatest comfort, and sprayed that vanilla scent all around the room.

> *What a wonderful way to enter heaven . . . with those you love, who love you too, massaging your feet and patting your hands.*

At one point in the last few days, the hospice nurse came for a visit and witnessed the crowd of leg rubbers and hair smoothers. "It's too much," she exclaimed. "Nancy needs her rest!"

Kathy looked at her amazed. "What *for?*" she asked.

I confess I had a moment, too, when I thought, is this—are we—too much? But then I decided what a wonderful way to enter heaven . . . with those you love, who love you too, massaging your feet and patting your hands.

Finally, she slipped into a semicoma, from which she murmured over and over, "Yes, yes, yes, yes," off and on for hours, sometimes shouting it loudly. *Tell me what you're seeing*, I thought.

She died on Sunday, in her little bedroom, five days before Molly and I needed to leave. Out of deference to their mom, I'm sure, and also for our sake, Johnny and Kathy planned the service for Wednesday so Molly could sing as Nancy requested, and I, too, could participate. God answered *all* our prayers.

a face in the cloud

I have touched two dead people: Nancy and my mother. That's it. It really doesn't matter how many dead bodies you see on television—it's not the same. Even with the sweet love that came from these women, it took awhile to replace those last wasted-away images in my mind with living ones. Though it was hard, I'm glad for every moment I spent in their sickrooms. In a way, it was my tribute.

At 3:00 Sunday morning I got the call. Sad and relieved, peaceful yet jittery with the early hour and the *meaning*, I drove to Nancy's place. Vicki, Jennie, and I clustered at Nancy's feet, holding hands, praying, musing over the earthly body of this dear friend of ours. It was an eerie moment.

"Could you dress her?" Kathy asked timidly, watching our faces. We picked out one of Nancy's favorite outfits, and then she quietly left us to the task. Jennie, a doctor's daughter, faced this situation like a medical professional, though she's not one. Vicki, who usually does what she has to do without complaining, didn't give herself the luxury of any external or internal discussion, as far as I know. I was the reluctant one, not afraid of the sight but a little leery of the feel of this friend, mentor, surrogate mother of mine.

a face in the cloud

I regret, but not too deeply, that we did not look for her teeth and set them back in her mouth as we had promised.

Sometimes death is not so bad. When you get to be a part of the dying process, when you're there day after day rubbing legs and feet, when you're familiar with where the extra sweater lives and how to empty the urine bag, when you know how to fluff the pillows just right and how long that yogurt's been in the refrigerator, the final moments of life are not so frightening. They're part of the scheme of things; they're the norm, the expected, the next step.

That's when death is aptly defined as bittersweet. There's no denying the sorrow, the loss, but it's such a sweet privilege to be there. And when the dying one is anticipating a reunion in heaven, and the face-to-face meeting of her God and Savior, and when you believe it, too, there is little to mourn.

> *Sometimes death is not so bad. When you get to be a part of the dying process, the final moments of life are not so frightening.*

Nancy's last party was her memorial service on a beautiful Wednesday in April. I intentionally wore my lime green sweater because she loved it. I could imagine her eyes crinkled in laughter and relief, there being no more pain and sadness in heaven. Molly, Jennie's daughter Lissie, and Vicki's son, Daniel, participated in the music. There was plenty of sniffling going on, but we all knew she would rather we not cry, so we sat there clutching our Kleenex, feeling at once guilty and rebellious.

> *I couldn't shake the feeling that Nancy was watching, listening to what was said about her. I even bet she was smiling with a mouthful of perfect teeth.*

The New Testament book of Hebrews says we have a great cloud of witnesses in heaven, followers of Christ who give evidence to God's sustaining presence and who might just be cheering us on as we live out our faith here on earth. Never before has that felt so real to me. Jennie, Vicki, and I couldn't shake the feeling that Nancy was watching, a face in the cloud, maybe straddling the steel beams high above us with Lynn at her side, like Huck Finn and Tom Sawyer, and peering down at our heads, listening to what was said about her. And I even bet she was smiling with a mouthful of perfect teeth.

She left specific instructions that there be no eulogies, so Ray the pastor shared a few life stories and then Jennie, Vicki, and I read some of her writing. She wouldn't have minded that. A writer loves to be read.

We adjourned to a festive luncheon in the fellowship hall of our church—chocolate had a prominent role at all the food stations—where many who loved her took the opportunity to write out a short tribute on half sheets of paper, especially designed for that purpose, that Kathy took home.

A few days later Nancy's family scattered her ashes in the ocean among a flotilla of small craft, the likes of which she knew so well. In that way she joined Lynn, who was also scattered in their beloved sea. But Kathy saved a few ashes and carried them to her home in northern California to bury beneath a dogwood in her yard.

A week after her death, Vicki, Jennie, and I received cards in the mail from Kathy and Johnny on behalf of their mom. Before she died, Nancy had arranged for each of us to receive a thousand-dollar gift certificate to Nordstrom's. She always loved a good splurge.

perfecting the art of love

One night a few months after Nancy died, as Jennie waited on a bench at a restaurant for Bob, a young family with an active toddler came in and sat across from her. Jennie loves to connect with children, and she's not inordinately shy with adults, but it is not her nature to go beyond small kindnesses and limited interaction on the street. Yet this time she said a sort of Nancy-presence hovered over her, and because of that she made a conscious effort to extend herself and to engage the family in conversation. In that short time a small human attachment was created, the toddler was climbing in *her* lap, and she felt that in some small way she was carrying on Nancy's work.

Maybe that very same day, though we're not sure, as I took my daily walk praying for my husband and kids, I saw half a block ahead a young teenager standing in her driveway waiting for her school bus. I thought to myself, *I should pray for her too. I bet she's going to my kids' alma mater.* That was fine, but as I got closer to her, I got a sense that, as long as I was going to walk right in front of her, maybe I should just ask her what to pray for.

Now, I am not afraid of fourteen-year-old girls waiting for school buses, but as soon as I had made that decision, I got a little nervous, wondering what she'd think about this strange woman, whom she wouldn't be able to avoid, talking to her about prayer. But I'd been writing about Nancy. And it seemed the right thing to do; actually, it seemed the only thing to do, that it would even be wrong to pass her without speaking after I'd had these thoughts.

So I walked up to her and said, "You may think this is strange, but I was praying for my kids and when I saw you, I thought I should pray for you too. And then I thought I might as well ask you what to pray for." Her somber expression brightened a little . . . I think. I pressed her gently for a specific request, and she said, "That I would be more comfortable talking to people." Her name was Cassie, and her mother's name was Mary; she did, indeed, go to my kids' high school. So much in common. I promised to pray that she'd talk to two people she didn't normally connect with that day, and I did pray for a good five minutes as I continued up the hill, where I came upon another timid freshman, Colin, clutching and kneading his baseball cap, who was afraid he'd just missed his bus. I went into my spiel, telling him I'd decided to pray for every lone teenager I passed that morning, and I asked him, "What can I pray for you?" He seemed quite relieved that he could get his need off his chest. "That the bus that just went by wasn't mine!"

Right there, out loud, I prayed, and his bus came down the street when we opened our eyes.

Would I have stopped without Nancy's spirit so alive in my head? Would I have stopped if I hadn't just been writing about her? Who knows. But two lonely kids—and one young family—

153

had encounters with moms who walked just a few steps out of their comfort zones.

I am a servant to my comfort zones. I like them nice and tidy and ever undisturbed. When they're threatened, so am I. Here I am fifty-six years old and hesitant to get involved in the lives around me, happier with a good book and a soft chair than with any of the messy stress that comes with people.

But I'm growing uncomfortable in "the zone," as much as I hate to admit it. I cannot, in all good conscience, shut myself away like I might want. I'm too aware of the importance of life, of the passing of time, of the possible missing of the purpose God is setting before me. It's not a guilt thing; it's an awareness thing.

> *God doesn't look at me and say, "Shame, shame, shame!" But rather, "Let's go for it this time, OK?"*

I've been reading about life-wasting, thinking about how I spend my time. On the day when I stand before the Lord, what will I have to show for my life? A long, industrious reading list of the great novels of the twentieth century?

It sends chills up and down my spine to imagine such a scene. I know I've missed countless opportunities to be there for someone, to listen, to carry groceries, to counsel, to admonish, to pray, to baby-sit, to encourage, to teach, to touch, to hug, to love.

But this is also what I know—that God doesn't look at me

and say, "Shame, shame, shame!" But rather, "Let's go for it *this* time, OK?"

I once asked Nancy if she had one thing she would like to say to older women, maybe to the people in retirement centers, what would it be?

"For Pete's sake," she exclaimed, "get up off your backside and go do something for somebody else, someone who doesn't do anything necessarily for you! Get off the tack of 'what's in it for me.' *It's not about you.*"

I was surprised to hear her so heated up. She went on. "How many of these women have held a child on their lap in the last month and read to them? There are so many needs out there. These people can't wait to get the calendar to see what's there for them this month. 'Oh goody, I get to go here, I get to go there, I get to go to the other place.' Well, it's not about them. I can't quite explain it. I just feel sad for people in general who do not reach out to other people. If I were younger, I would want to start an organization of reaching out."

"What would you do?" I asked her.

"I don't know. I wouldn't know where to start, except to encourage people to reach out to somebody, anybody. You can't believe how a guy out there sweeping the streets, how his face will light up when I stop to talk to him for a minute. You know, it's made his whole day. For just a minute he's risen above whatever it is he's doing."

"Do you ever find it hard to do that?"

"Never! I don't even think about it. It's as automatic as scratching an itch."

Sometimes I wonder what it is exactly that God calls us to. With all the talk of purpose-driven lives, what exactly does that mean in the context of the daily lives that most of us live? In the process of determining our gifts, finding our calling, charting our personality, what should we be doing day after day after day?

Without classifying her as the poster child of purposeful living, I think Nancy had it right on. Real ministry is living out the life of Christ among the relationships He has put around us. Some of us are called to obvious ministry, the kind of formal calling your mind goes to when people use that word. But all of us, even those we call ministers or missionaries or speakers or Bible study leaders, have to perfect the art of love.

Nancy was passionate about it. I can be passionate about it on paper, but it's a learning curve to work it out with every single face I see. But it's what I want, and I know it's what God wants as well.

There's something very satisfying in knowing that God's and my plans match up.

"supermentorwoman"

One day, in the spirit of reaching out, Vicki suggested that she and I take on a couple of younger women in an informal "older woman/younger woman" relationship. The word *mentor* was thrown about here and there, but I put the brakes on that. I didn't want to raise anyone's expectations. I had to say yes though. My years with Nancy were so heavy on my mind that this seemed to be the logical next step. So Vicki paired up with Molly, and I took on Jennie's daughter, Jordan.

Jordan was one of Nancy's favorite projects. They met when Jordan was a child, and Nancy became a sounding board for her through some pretty rough years. She provided a positive perspective and modeled an enthusiasm about life, fronted her the money for a much-needed car, and when Jordan's son, Micah, came along, Nancy was smitten. But mostly Nancy and Jordan were soul mates. I know Jordan misses her to this day.

Jordan is a late-twenties single mom dealing with stuff in her life I've never experienced. I couldn't imagine she'd be even remotely interested in meeting with me—we have so little in common—but she, too, acquiesced to Vicki's suggestion. One

June morning we sat down together at Starbucks and had a chat. I can't tell you how nervous I was. I should have gone decaf.

We decided right up front to go through a book together, one for women that was making the rounds in our church. I had no other idea of how to relate to her and so little experience with such encounters that it seemed the safest route.

Every week we discussed a chapter. It was a book of deep themes that caused us to talk rather freely about experiences and reactions we may never have shared before—certainly never shared with an unknown commodity like we were to each other. We talked about dreams and fears, about trust and love, and weekly we exposed more and more of our inner selves.

> I am not proud that I'm becoming this "Starbucks listening post." I'm grateful.

Some days we had amazing discussions, and other days one or both of us was in the dumps. But we kept going and going and going. Fifty lattés later we're still meeting. Our relationship has developed to the point of trust and love and truthfulness—she is like my daughter, and I am another woman in her life who probably says what her mother would say but through an unrelated pair of lips.

Meeting with Jordan has opened me up. Though sometimes I feel like I'm nothing but a sounding board, and at times not even that, and though our lives look so different and I really *can't* relate on some levels, I think I'm giving her one more place to test her dreams and cement her faith. That right there brings meaning to my life.

As soon as Jordan and I began meeting, interesting little encounters popped up here and there, people that God put in my path, other young women with whom I deliberately decided to engage. I even have a regular table at Starbucks.

I am not proud that I'm becoming this "Starbucks listening post." I'm grateful. Grateful that God is allowing me to be that fleshed-out ambassador of His, grateful that He's setting up the situations, grateful that He's promised to speak through me so the onus is not on me to be wise. I continue to stumble through these encounters, but I'm learning . . . though sometimes I wish He'd write it on a napkin right in front of my face.

Speaking of which, I met a teenager for coffee the other day. We were introduced a couple of weeks before, and I was high on Jordan. I hate to reveal my motivations, and, really, I have no idea what they are half the time, but there is a possibility that I was thinking, *I've got this mentoring thing going on, and wouldn't this young girl like a little time with someone like me?*

I was tired when we met—no excuse—but somehow it just didn't go well. I groped for advice, searched my mind for questions, and pleaded silently while looking out the window for God to give me wisdom. "God? God? Hel-lo-oh. I'm sitting here staring out this window, waiting for a little he-lp . . ."

I went home discouraged and ate a pint of mint chocolate-chip ice cream in front of the TV.

But in the morning God encouraged me with reminders that I should continue to step out and that He'll take care of it. That He rewards faithfulness and can use any aging mother to accomplish His purpose. It was one of those mornings I felt spoken to, encouraged, chosen to receive a particular message.

It's so tempting to form a picture of what a mentor looks like and says and does. There is reason to have such a picture in more formal situations. What I don't want to get in the habit of doing, though, is deciding for myself what a mentor should look like and then coming to the conclusion that it doesn't look like me, so I shouldn't be faithful, available, teachable.

I don't think Nancy would have considered herself a mentor, though women asked her to be that for them. I think she just responded to a need. She probably had a friend who needed to talk, or met a young person who intrigued her or reminded her of herself, or was introduced to a new writer who needed a little direction. She knew she could listen. She knew she had a way of turning situations around so the positive perspective came out on top.

I don't know what my life is going to include down the road. I just know I can't bear the thought of having no impact on anyone's life, of becoming a little old lady inside as well as outside. It scares me to think that younger women might depend on me to direct them. I almost want to delete all this mentoring stuff so no one expects it of me. It scares me to begin a relationship that could go on for a long time. As I said, I'd rather read a book.

But not really. I know my hobbies are not how I want my life to be defined. Maybe this really does all go back to Nancy's hot buttons: *get your eyes off yourself, keep a positive attitude, pour your life into others.* Maybe as I turn my focus outward, away from myself and away from the fear of failure—not to be some "super-mentorwoman" but just to be a friend—maybe I will be a positive force in other lives like Nancy was in mine.

This is the thing: I must be open to trying and to failing, to succeeding and to letting go. I'm sure I'll do this over and over, get together with someone, old or young, and not quite connect. Even Nancy didn't click with everyone. Yet it's got to be worth the risk. Somewhere down the line I'll be able to get myself out of the way, and it will finally sink in that it's not about me.

I just want to be faithful . . . and available . . . and teachable. And someday when I'm lying in an adjustable bed, I want bunches of friends to massage my feet.

tell me what you see

There are living people who are dead on the inside and dead people who continue to live on in the lives of others. Photographs and videos, memories and mementos keep them alive. But the most lasting legacy is a passed-down *life*—replete with values, convictions, character, and love.

From day one—for some odd, prideful reason—I couldn't acknowledge that Nancy might be a mentor for me. I didn't want to idolize her, to have an agenda for our relationship, to set her up on some sort of pedestal. She didn't like pedestals. I wanted her as a friend, and if God had a deeper purpose in mind for us, I wasn't going to hunt for it. He could bring it to light if He so chose.

So He did.

In simple terms, Nancy helped me live and I helped her die. I definitely got the sweeter deal.

Our friendship made us better. God gave Nancy someone to write with and one more friend to take her places, even into death, and He put me in the way of this unique woman who made me face some of my greater weaknesses.

Isn't that amazing? How wonderful to be the recipient of

such attention to detail. How wonderful to be loved enough to be confronted.

The beauty of a good friendship is just that—it moves us beyond casual association to a point of accountability and change. There's a price you pay to be and to have a good friend. It's time consuming and heart consuming, and sometimes it takes some dying.

So how goes your attitude these days? you ask. *Are you "too laid back to get out of bed"?* I have to admit that all this focus and reflection have made an indelible mark on my mind and on my actions. I have a much deeper conviction now that it's useless and wasteful to worry, that I don't have enough energy anyway, so why spend the little I have worrying over things I can't control? I believe that worry is not just a little annoyance but an actual besetting sin that God would like me to let go of.

I'm also finding that more of my immediate thoughts are positive ones—or at least more neutral—as

> *The most lasting legacy is a passed-down life—replete with values, convictions, character, and love.*

Nancy promised they'd be by now. And I'm much more aware of the need to get my eyes off myself and onto others, so I'm getting better at it. This is what happens when you focus on an issue and talk about it and write about it and even debate it with friends. God takes all that input, uses all those influences, to bring you around to a greater understanding of yourself, the issue, and Him.

And you know what I've learned about growing old? It just happens. It's a stage of *life*, not a prelude to death. It's not something to fear or avoid or mask with hair color (though I do); it's a time of giving and returning and, yes, growing. It's a time of opportunity, and the sooner baby-boomers like me decide to use that time rather than lose it, the better off we and our kids and grandkids will be. God doesn't waste anything, and we shouldn't either.

And really, bottom line, isn't it all about God and what He wants? Isn't it really about letting go of what might disturb us and letting Him do His healing thing, His renewing work? Someday we *will* stand before Him and give an account of how we handled our lives. Of whether we lived in fear or victory, in defeat or joy, for ourselves or others. I much prefer the idea of facing Him with a smile on my face. And I like the idea that Nancy will get part of the credit for it.

By the way, you might be wondering if Nancy turned introspective by the time she died. Let's just say she dabbled in it more than she ever believed she would.

Nancy and I began writing our book on a hillside overlooking the Pacific. We wanted to explore our friendship and the joy we found in each other's company. When, finally, we had to admit, even embrace, the subject of death . . . well, even then we wanted to focus on the fun stuff. Or perhaps we lacked the discipline to write any other way.

In fact, our writing suffered because the sky was too blue, the breeze just perfect, the road always beckoning.

Nancy and I had a simple friendship, and only for about five years. I really didn't expect to be writing this book on my own; I didn't expect to have a traveling companion who didn't share my surname; I didn't expect to be part of a death watch. But God has a way of framing our lives apart from our expectations. I suppose our job is to not be so surprised.

I doubt I'll ever find another older friend who will call me "darling," or cradle my head in her lap as if I were her child, or who will delight in the trivial parts of my children's lives and mine—although if there's anything Nancy taught me, it's to *look* for people like that, to not be afraid to get involved and entwined in another life.

> God has a way of framing our lives apart from our expectations. I suppose our job is to not be so surprised.

And I doubt I'll ever find another car-trip companion as ready to go, as available, and as agreeable as she was. As long as we stopped for ice cream, she was happy.

Nancy had a bundle of flaws just like the rest of us. Now and then she could be stubborn and demanding, and occasionally she traded tact for an in-your-face directness that could sting. But that's not what I'll remember. Her face will come to mind when I'm confronted with a challenge and tempted to talk my way out of it. I'll think of her when I find myself giving in to fear or dwelling on the past. Or when a young mother needs a friend. Pecans and Gouda will remind me of her. And maps.

Knowing Nancy didn't change my personality, erase my innate shyness, dissolve my hesitancy, or heal my self-esteem issues. She didn't *transform* me, except in the ways we are all transformed by the people we know and love. But she made me uncomfortable with the patterns of thinking I'd adopted. And she alerted me, flashed a warning light. "Watch out! Don't miss that person! Don't miss this life!"

I got the message. I hope Nancy's watching, listening, reading this over my shoulder. I hope she's proud of how I'm handling my life without her, proud that her example is staying with me, that I'm learning my lessons. I hope she likes the book and has noticed that I finished this journey without as much angst as I began. Tell me what you see, Nancy.

epilogue:
for lynn on his birthday—

gulfito, costa rica
august 9, 1975
by nancy bayless

I'd like
To tell you
How I feel (after thinking it over)
About this thing
So very real
That happened
To my life
The day
You decided
You would stay
And take my heart
Off of the beach
To have forever
In your reach
It's hard sometimes

167

what an old friend taught me about life

To put in words
The freedom of
The flying birds
You have to sit
With eyes raised high
And watch them float
Across the sky
The same is true
With me for you
I pinch myself
To know you're true
And then there comes
My evening star
A quiet brilliance
From afar
I feel the same thing
In your arms
Surrounded by your
Precious charms
And then there is
Our "Apogee"
You made a lovely
Home for me
A place where we
Can love or rest
A place to live
The daily test

epilogue: for lynn on his birthday—

Of truth and faith
And what is best
For us to do
Within our days
A place to think up
All the ways
To show our love
To one another
To never for a
Moment smother
Any thought
Or crazy dream
That wanders
Like a running stream
Across the mind
Of either two
A place to know
When day is through
You mean the same
As I
To you.
Happy Birthday

journal

journal

journal

journal

journal

journal

journal

journal

journal

journal

Mary Jenson will tell you her biggest claims to fame are her thirty-five-year marriage to husband, Ron, and their two grown children who, unlike so many of their friends, really love spending time together as a family. It wasn't until she neared the empty nest time in her life that she entered the writing life; since then she has published three books and has partnered with her husband in some of his writing endeavors. Together they speak for Family-Life marriage conferences. Mary serves on the board of the San Diego Christian Writers Guild and works with Moms In Touch International.